"All Scripture is inspired by God and is useful for teaching the truth, rebuking error, correcting faults, and giving instructions for right living, so that the person who serves God may be fully qualified and equipped to do every kind of good deed."

2 Timothy 3:16-17
Good News Bible

Sunday Gospel Readings
with *Lectio Divina*
Year C: Year of Luke

"The Roman Catholic Bishops of Scotland once more recommend this resource for the prayerful reading of the word of God. The 2008 Synod of Bishops in Rome had as its theme the word of God and *Lectio Divina* was recognised, described and recommended as an important expression of the Church's love of Sacred Scripture (see the Message to the People of God, 9). The Bishops are grateful to the Scottish Bible Society and all those who have worked to produce this volume based on the readings for Year C of the Lectionary."

Catholic Bishops' Conference of Scotland

SCOTTISH
BIBLE SOCIETY
*Celebrating 200 years
taking the Word to the World*

These *Lectio Divina* outlines are also available in Albanian, Dutch, French, Greek, Maltese, Portuguese, Slovak, Slovenian, Spanish and other languages. For full details visit **www.wordforliving.org**

Acknowledgement: Thanks to the American Bible Society www.americanbible.org for
granting permission to adapt material from *Encuentro Con La Biblia/Encounter With the
Bible* for use in the introduction.

For enquiries: info@ubs-europe.org

INTRODUCTION

These weekly outlines combine the Liturgy's Sunday Gospel readings with the *lectio divina* approach to Holy Scripture.

Lectio divina is a dynamic, life-oriented approach to reading Holy Scriptures encouraged by both Pope John Paul II and Pope Benedict XVI. It provides a framework for a faithful and respectful reading of the Bible that is sincere and authentic.

Lectio divina is a blessing for the entire Church as it opens up the rich truths of Scripture for every Christian. Through it believers are invited to read, understand and deepen their appreciation of the Scriptures and to seek guidance for their lives in the teaching of the Lord Jesus.

Our real goal is to meet our Lord as we read his Word and allow him to transform our lives to be more like him through the work of the Holy Spirit.

All the information necessary for you to have a meaningful encounter with God's Word is included in this booklet. These outlines can be used individually or in groups.

The following pages introduce the four steps of *lectio divina* with some extra tips for using these outlines in groups.

ABOUT LECTIO DIVINA

History

Lectio divina dates back to the early Church Fathers around 300 AD. The four steps were first recorded by a monk, Guigo Cartujo, in 1173. These steps Lectio (Reading), Meditatio (Meditation), Oratio (Prayer) and Contemplatio (Contemplation) remain central today although methods differ.

Overview

In essence *lectio divina* is a simple way to meet with the Lord through reflection and prayer based on Holy Scripture. It is not a study method. Background knowledge can be helpful but is not essential.

Used in groups a structure is necessary but for individuals the steps need not be followed rigidly. Our aim is meeting God, not just completing the steps themselves. So when the Lord impresses something on us we need to stop and wait. We can always come back to the steps another time. We don't want to lose what God is saying to us.

LECTIO – READING

Reading the Scripture passage humbly and prayerfully is the foundation for everything else that follows and cannot be rushed. So begin with a prayer and ask the Holy Spirit to 'lead you into all the truth' (John 16:13).

Read the passage slowly and carefully. Avoid being tempted to look at the Lectio comments or any of the other steps at this stage.

Have a notebook and pencil ready. Underline, or make a note of, any words or phrases that stand out to you. Write down any questions that occur to you. Read the passage several times and read it aloud. Give yourself time to understand and appreciate what is being said.

Now read the Lectio comments and reflect on the ways they are similar or different to your first thoughts.

 # MEDITATIO – MEDITATION

Meditation deepens our appreciation of the passage and helps us to explore its riches. We read in 2 Timothy 3:16 that 'All Scripture is inspired by God and is useful for teaching the truth, rebuking error, correcting faults, and giving instructions for right living…' So approach Scripture in faith expecting God to speak to you. He may reveal something of himself to you. He might highlight an attitude or behaviour of yours that needs to change. He might show you a promise to encourage and strengthen you.

Here are some suggested approaches you may find helpful.

Use your imagination. Picture the passage; put yourself into the scene and become part of the story. See things through the eyes of the other characters, listen to what they say, watch their reactions, imagine how they feel. Keep coming back to Jesus. Get to know him; delight yourself and become fascinated by him, his words, his actions, the way he responds – everything about him.

Ask questions. Use your own questions and the questions given to think more deeply about the passage and what God wants to say to you. Ask Jesus why he did and said what he did. Try to understand his reasons and intentions. Allow time to be quiet, to listen and hear his answer.

Let the Word be a mirror for you. As we read the Bible it shows us more of what the Christian life looks like and where ours needs to change. We see how God's Word applies to our daily life, as an individual, and as part of our community and society. We will find promises and encouragement, challenges and demands. If we are willing God will nurture and free us to be more fully human and fully alive.

ORATIO – PRAYER

Prayer opens up a conversation between God and us. In the Psalms we see how the writers pour out their feelings to God, often mixing hopes and fears side by side. God values our honesty. We can't hide anything from him anyway. Using the words of the responsorial psalm can help us but we can also use our own words to have a heart-to-heart conversation with a very special friend.

Through prayer we make our response to the light God's Word has shed on how we are living our lives. Now we can bring what is happening in our own life and in our community before God. We speak and listen, listen and reflect – it is a conversation with God.

 ## CONTEMPLATIO – CONTEMPLATION:

To help us interpret the Gospel reading the Liturgy provides two further Scripture readings. Reflecting on these can both enrich our understanding of the text and bring into focus a response we may need to make to the Lord.

Contemplation gives us the opportunity for an intimate time of communion with God. Be still before God and invite him in. Few words, if any, are necessary here. Enjoy time in his presence. Just be with him and let him love you. Let him refresh your soul.

Review

After you have finished your time of reading, meditation, prayer and contemplation you may want to jot down in a notebook any experiences or thoughts that particularly impressed you. You may find it helpful to look back at these later.

USING THESE OUTLINES IN GROUPS

When *lectio divina* is used in a group a little preparation is needed.

 LECTIO:

Try one or more of the following ways of reading the passage. See what works best for your particular group.

Individual reading. To start with give everyone time to read through the passage silently.

Proclamation of the Word. One person reads (proclaims) the Word. This is the traditional manner of reading in the liturgical celebration.

Two readers. Two people read the text aloud alternately.

Each person reads a verse. This is a way of involving each participant, inviting each to read from his own Bible, so that the reading is attentive and dynamic.

Audio version. If you have access to a recorded version of the text you could also use that. You may notice different words are stressed.

With different characters. Approach the text somewhat like a drama, in which one person is the narrator/reader, another takes the part of Jesus, a third takes another character. This can be the most dynamic or engaging method and helps us to identify just what the different characters in the passage are saying.

 MEDITATIO:

- In the group setting, it is important that everyone is given time to participate, to share what the Lord has been saying to them. While the Lord speaks through his Word, he also speaks to us through our brothers and sisters. So as we listen to others we need to open our hearts to hear the Lord's voice speaking through them.

- It is important that everyone in the group understands that this sharing is to build one another up and enrich our experience. It is not necessary that everyone agrees about what is shared. You need to be careful to avoid this time turning into a debate or argument. The Lord knows us each as individuals so will have different things to say to us personally at this specific point in our lives.

- You can start with a simple question like "What catches your attention in this passage?" and use the printed questions. The aim is to help everyone feel comfortable to speak and share how the text has inspired them. Gently keep the group focused on the text and what God is saying.

ORATIO:

We suggest you give people time for personal silent prayer before God. You can also give opportunity for people to pray out loud in their own words and use verses from the responsorial prayer. The aim should be to help each person make a personal response to the Lord during this time.

 CONTEMPLATIO:

Contemplation by its very nature is an individual exercise and silence is necessary. If you have room it may be helpful to suggest people move so they have their own 'personal space'.

The Scripture references for the Psalms follow the Hebrew numbering used in many recent Bibles including the Jerusalem Bible but some Bibles use different numbering. If Psalm 23 The Good Shepherd is numbered as Psalm 22 in your Bible, please refer to your church lectionary for all the correct Psalm references for your Bible.

WATCH AND PRAY

Luke 21:25-28, 34-36

[25] "There will be strange things happening to the sun, the moon, and the stars. On earth whole countries will be in despair, afraid of the roar of the sea and the raging tides. [26] People will faint from fear as they wait for what is coming over the whole earth, for the powers in space will be driven from their courses. [27] Then the Son of Man will appear, coming in a cloud with great power and glory. [28] When these things begin to happen, stand up and raise your heads, because your salvation is near."

[34] "Be on your guard! Don't let yourselves become occupied with too much feasting and drinking and with the worries of this life, or that Day may suddenly catch you [35] like a trap. For it will come upon all people everywhere on earth. [36] Be on the alert and pray always that you will have the strength to go safely through all those things that will happen and to stand before the Son of Man."

Other Readings: Jeremiah 33:14-16; *Psalm 25:4-5, 8-9, 10, 14; 1 Thessalonians 3:12-4:2

 LECTIO:

Advent opens with a vivid teaching from Jesus on what the days preceding his second coming will be like. The words are taken from Jesus' teaching ministry in Jerusalem following his public entry.

Jesus' teaching ministry did two things. It challenged the Jewish authorities who refused to recognise God's action in what Jesus said and did. It also reached out to the Jewish crowds who flocked after him wherever he went.

Apparently Jesus had decided to reserve some teachings for his inner group – the disciples. The verses above were for his disciples' ears only. Jesus is speaking about the end days when the world as we know it will cease. Scholars use the technical term 'eschatological' to describe this sort of teaching.

This collapse of the world as we know it will be terrifying. Jesus doesn't underestimate people's reaction either; most will panic and be terrified. But, and

---

*See note at the end of the Introduction on the previous page.

it is a big but, Jesus tells his disciples they have nothing to fear from these terrible events. He explains why - because when these things happen they will know their 'salvation is near'.

In this madness people will still be struggling to survive. But for Jesus' disciples it will be a time of liberation. There is just one proviso - the disciples must be on the alert. Jesus wants to find them prepared, ready. And we too must stay alert and keep our focus on Jesus in the midst of the busyness and temptations of everyday life.

 # MEDITATIO:

- How can we balance 'waiting for the Lord to come' alongside a godly enjoyment of all the good things human life offers?
- Compare the different responses of the people in verse 26 with those in verse 28. What will help us respond like the faithful people in verse 28?
- How can Jesus help us with the worries of life? Does 1 Peter 5:7 help us?
- How prepared do you feel for Jesus' return, say tomorrow? What might help you? Jesus gives us some guidance in verses 34 and 36.

 # ORATIO:

Today's passage teaches us that prayer is vital in preparation for Jesus' return. The verses selected from today's Psalm remind us that God is righteous and good. He will guide us if we are willing to listen and he is a friend to all who obey him.

Read through these verses several times. Let God convince you of his love and care. Ask him to help make verses 4 and 5 your own prayer:

'Teach me your ways, O Lord;
make them known to me.
Teach me to live according to your truth,
For you are my God, who saves me.
I always trust in you.'

 # CONTEMPLATIO:

Ponder the phrase 'your salvation is near' and what this means to you.

Contemplate Jesus returning to earth 'with great power and glory', and the joy he will share with everyone who loves him.

PREPARING THE WAY FOR JESUS

Luke 3:1-6

[1] It was the fifteenth year of the rule of the Emperor Tiberius; Pontius Pilate was governor of Judea, Herod was ruler of Galilee, and his brother Philip was ruler of the territory of Iturea and Trachonitis; Lysanias was ruler of Abilene, [2] and Annas and Caiaphas were high priests. At that time the word of God came to John son of Zechariah in the desert. [3] So John went throughout the whole territory of the River Jordan, preaching, "Turn away from your sins and be baptized, and God will forgive your sins."

[4] As it is written in the book of the prophet Isaiah:
"Someone is shouting in the desert:
  'Get the road ready for the Lord;
  make a straight path for him to travel!
[5] Every valley must be filled up,
  every hill and mountain levelled off.
The winding roads must be made straight,
  and the rough paths made smooth.
[6] The whole human race will see God's salvation!' "

Other Readings: Baruch 5:1-9; Psalm 126; Philippians 1:3-6, 8-11

 LECTIO:

Luke wants people to be able to pin down the exact period of time he is talking about. He sees John the Baptist rooted in reality as he briefly moves centre stage. John's story begins to unfold in Luke 1 and 2.

Every Jew would have known about Tiberius the Roman emperor because Palestine was under Roman rule. Pontius Pilate, the local Roman ruler, had been notorious and they would probably have known about the various Herodian governors, or kings. The names of the high priests, Ananias and Caiaphas, would have also been instantly recognizable.

Here, in this inflammatory political situation of Roman occupation, John began his God-given ministry in the Jordan valley. He preached a message of repentance and baptism. Those who were willing, and there were many, repented of their sins and were baptized publicly in the river Jordan.

Luke makes a link between John's ministry and a prophecy in the Book of Isaiah about a voice 'shouting in the desert'. In Isaiah it refers to the return of the exiled Jews, from Babylon to their homeland. John's ministry points to Jesus and prepares the way for him.

Luke sees a two-fold meaning in this prophetic link. Not only is John proclaiming a way home for the 'exiles'. His voice 'shouting in the desert' is also a chance for humankind to prepare their sinful, unreceptive and barren hearts for Jesus' ministry. How? By 'smoothing the path' and repenting of their sins.

 MEDITATIO:

- Imagine you have been forced to live in another country, and as a slave too. What might your feelings be? What would be top of your prayer list?
- Why do you think it was so important for Luke to link John's ministry to historical people and events?
- John's ministry was to prepare the way for people to meet Jesus. How can we prepare the way for people to meet Jesus today? What obstacles might people have and how can we help?

 ORATIO:

Psalm 126 is a psalm of thanksgiving for past deliverance and a plea for help. Thank God that our sins can be forgiven and praise him for the times he has rescued you in the past.

Pray for those needing special help now. If these are hard times for you, perhaps you can ask someone to pray for you too?

Join Isaiah in praying that 'the whole human race will see God's salvation'. Pray especially for people that you know.

 CONTEMPLATIO:

The reading from Philippians offers a rich seam of joyful hope – make the promises there your own. During the coming week reflect on the Day of Christ and our hope of meeting Jesus when his work in us is complete. Ask God to shape your life so he brings glory to himself.

LIVING RIGHT

Luke 3:10-18

¹⁰ The people asked him, "What are we to do, then?"

¹¹ He answered, "Whoever has two shirts must give one to the man who has none, and whoever has food must share it."

¹² Some tax collectors came to be baptized, and they asked him, "Teacher, what are we to do?"

¹³ "Don't collect more than is legal," he told them.

¹⁴ Some soldiers also asked him, "What about us? What are we to do?"

He said to them, "Don't take money from anyone by force or accuse anyone falsely. Be content with your pay."

¹⁵ People's hopes began to rise, and they began to wonder whether John perhaps might be the Messiah. ¹⁶ So John said to all of them, "I baptize you with water, but someone is coming who is much greater than I am. I am not good enough even to untie his sandals. He will baptize you with the Holy Spirit and fire. ¹⁷ He has his winnowing shovel with him, to thresh out all the grain and gather the wheat into his barn; but he will burn the chaff in a fire that never goes out."

¹⁸ In many different ways John preached the Good News to the people and urged them to change their ways.

Other Readings: Zephaniah 3:14-18; Isaiah 12:2-6; Philippians 4:4-7

 LECTIO:

Week by week Luke leads us through John's ministry. Now the final tragic conclusion in Herod's prison looms.

But first Luke reveals John's ministry to the different people who sought peace of mind and a way forward. He gave direct instructions.

The hated tax collectors, for example, are told not to abuse their power. In John's day, provided the Roman authorities received their taxes they turned a blind eye if the tax collectors took more for themselves. So tax collectors could effectively rob people and put the surplus cash in their own pockets. Many grew very rich doing so.

By contrast, soldiers were poorly paid. They used force to obtain things like extra food and money from people.

Neither situation was right. John preached a moral life and those who listened to him and accepted his teaching changed their lives.

People began to hope that John might be the long expected Messiah. John shattered their dream immediately by saying, 'someone is coming who is much greater than I am.' John described his mission as a preparation for the coming Messiah.

John also met Herod Antipas, who was keen to hear his teaching. Herod Antipas, one of Herod the Great's sons, had been appointed leader of the northern area of Galilee by the Romans. John, never one to hold back, was very direct in criticizing Herod Antipas' immoral lifestyle. Sadly, John's directness led to his arrest and imprisonment by Herod.

 MEDITATIO:

- Consider how the principles in John's teaching in verses 8 and 11-14 are relevant to us today. What stands out for you?
- Some people have more than they really need; others, not enough. How do you relate to verse 11?
- Verse 17 could strike terror in your heart until you remember Jesus is the Good News (the forgiveness of sins). What does the Good News mean for you and how do you balance it with verse 17?

 ORATIO:

Ask the Holy Spirit to use today's Gospel reading to reveal if there is anything you need to do or to change.

Read Isaiah 12:2-6 and Zephaniah 3:14-18 and make these great hymns of praise personal to you.

Praise God for the wonderful things he has done. Praise him for sending Jesus. Thank him for revealing his love for you and for the countless times he has helped you. Ask the Holy Spirit to help you tell others just how wonderful God is.

 CONTEMPLATIO:

Contemplate Jesus as Saviour and think of his redeeming grace opening the door to salvation for everyone who will accept him.

Consider Paul's wise advice in Philippians 4:4-7. Remember you can give God all your cares and worries in prayer; his peace will fill and protect your heart and mind.

JUMP FOR JOY

Luke 1:39-44

[39] Soon afterwards Mary got ready and hurried off to a town in the hill country of Judea. [40] She went into Zechariah's house and greeted Elizabeth. [41] When Elizabeth heard Mary's greeting, the baby moved within her. Elizabeth was filled with the Holy Spirit [42] and said in a loud voice, "You are the most blessed of all women, and blessed is the child you will bear! [43] Why should this great thing happen to me, that my Lord's mother comes to visit me? [44] For as soon as I heard your greeting, the baby within me jumped with gladness.

Other Readings: Micah 5:1-4; Psalm 80:1-2, 14-15, 17-18; Hebrews 10:5-10

 LECTIO:

With the angel Gabriel's amazing news of her cousin Elizabeth's unexpected pregnancy (Luke 1: 36) it didn't take Mary long to pack and set off for a visit. Now she had incredible news of her own.

With many of God's announcements and actions the full significance can be slow to dawn on the individuals involved. Abraham's wife Sarah laughed when she was told she would become a mother in old age (Genesis 18:12). Zechariah, Elizabeth's husband, doubted and was struck dumb throughout Elizabeth's pregnancy (Luke 1:20). Mary, whatever her own doubts and anxieties, simply accepted what God wanted, 'I am the Lord's servant, may it happen to me as you said' (Luke 1:38).

A shouted greeting announced Mary's arrival to Elizabeth, and caused a surprising thing to happen. Elizabeth's baby leapt in the womb. She was probably accustomed to the baby moving by now. The surprising thing was that the Holy Spirit caused the movement. And Elizabeth, filled with the Holy Spirit, 'recognises' and proclaims Mary as the mother of the Lord and blesses her in this role.

This short passage is often referred to as the Visitation. Not only is Mary visiting Elizabeth, but Jesus is making his first visit to 'his people'. John, still hidden within Elizabeth's womb, recognises Jesus as the Messiah and leaps for pure joy.

What a precious encounter it must have been for the two expectant mothers and the babies they carried. Such an encouragement to each of them. Mary's faith must have had a tremendous boost. As she blesses Mary, Elizabeth echoes the Angel Gabriel's words to Mary (Luke 1:28, 30-33).

MEDITATIO:

- Consider how Mary might have felt before and after her visit to see her cousin Elizabeth. On the one hand, there was Elizabeth's wonderful news after a lifetime of childlessness. But what would Elizabeth, wife of the priest Zechariah, make of Mary's news? Would she believe her or would she shun her?
- Filled with the Holy Spirit, Elizabeth speaks out and confirms Mary as the mother of the long-awaited Messiah. How might Mary have felt about these words? The verses following today's reading give a big clue (Luke 1:46-56).
- Consider the Holy Spirit's role in guiding Elizabeth and Mary. Have you experienced the Holy Spirit guiding you? What do you remember of these events?

 # ORATIO:

Psalm 80 is a heartfelt plea for God to restore the nation of Israel. Join the psalmist and cry out to the faithful Shepherd (God) to rescue the people you know who do not follow him.

Ask God to turn the hardened hearts of people in your country towards him. Sometimes our own hearts can do with a little softening in some areas too. God has promised to give us hearts of flesh to replace our hearts of stone (Ezekiel 11:19).

Ask God to help you recognise the leading of the Holy Spirit and for the faith and courage to obey his prompting.

 # CONTEMPLATIO:

God is often described as a shepherd. Contemplate the ways God shepherds you personally and then how he shepherds whole nations, when they allow him to do so.

Meditate on the title given to Jesus – Prince of Peace.

Micah's prophecy was given about 700 years before Jesus' birth. He was not the only one to prophesy Jesus' birth. Jeremiah announced it too around 150 years later. We read this in the Sunday readings three weeks ago (Jeremiah 33:14-16). Reflect on Micah's prophecy. What does it signify for you?

A SAVIOUR IS BORN FOR US

Luke 2:1-14

¹ At that time the Emperor Augustus ordered a census to be taken throughout the Roman Empire. ² When this first census took place, Quirinius was the governor of Syria. ³ Everyone, then, went to register himself, each to his own town.

⁴ Joseph went from the town of Nazareth in Galilee to the town of Bethlehem in Judea, the birthplace of King David. Joseph went there because he was a descendant of David. ⁵ He went to register with Mary, who was promised in marriage to him. She was pregnant, ⁶ and while they were in Bethlehem, the time came for her to have her baby. ⁷ She gave birth to her first son, wrapped him in strips of cloth and laid him in a manger – there was no room for them to stay in the inn.

⁸ There were some shepherds in that part of the country who were spending the night in the fields, taking care of their flocks. ⁹ An angel of the Lord appeared to them, and the glory of the Lord shone over them. They were terribly afraid, ¹⁰ but the angel said to them, "Don't be afraid! I am here with good news for you, which will bring great joy to all the people. ¹¹ This very day in David's town your Saviour was born – Christ the Lord! ¹² And this is what will prove it to you: you will find a baby wrapped in strips of cloth and lying in a manger."

¹³ Suddenly a great army of heaven's angels appeared with the angel, singing praises to God:

¹⁴ "Glory to God in the highest heaven,
   and peace on earth to those with
   whom he is pleased!"

Other Readings: Isaiah 9:1-7; Psalm 96:1-3, 11-13; Titus 2:11-14

 LECTIO:

The story of Jesus' birth is described in two scenes. In the first scene, verses 1-7, Luke explains how Jesus came to be born in Bethlehem, in the south of Palestine, when Mary and Joseph were living in Nazareth, in the north.

Joseph was required to attend a census. As a descendant of King David, that meant returning to Bethlehem. It is here that Mary gives birth to Jesus. God's promise that he would send the Messiah, a descendant of King David, is fulfilled (Isaiah 9:7). The place of Jesus' birth also fulfils Micah's prophecy (Micah 5:2).

In scene two, verses 8-14, we hear how the news of Jesus' birth reaches the outside world. Shepherds are the surprised recipients of the amazing news. God sends an angel to reveal the birth and real identity of this baby. The proof the angel gives the shepherds that this baby is God's promised Saviour is that they will find him in Bethlehem, lying in – of all places – an animals' feeding trough, a manger!

It's almost as if the angels can't contain their excitement at the birth of this child. For then suddenly a great army of angels join the first angel and sing their praise to God.

Our Scripture reading finishes here, but the story continues. The shepherds believe the news the angel tells them and go to Bethlehem to see for themselves. They find Jesus and tell Mary and Joseph everything the angel told them. They are the very first people to announce that Jesus is the long-awaited Saviour after his birth (verses 15-20).

 # MEDITATIO:

- Consider why God chose to reveal the birth of his son to shepherds, who in Jesus' day had a very low social status and were often considered as thieves.
- What clues do the circumstances of Jesus' birth give us that he would be a very different Messiah, and usher in a different kingdom, to the one people were expecting?
- Marvel that Jesus was prepared to leave the glory of heaven to be born as a baby in an animals' stable.
- Consider Jesus as your Saviour and Lord. What does this mean for you?

 # ORATIO:

Why not echo the words of the angelic army on that very first Christmas day: 'Glory to God in the highest heaven'? Repeat this great proclamation of praise several times.

Thank God for sending Jesus as your Saviour.

Remember those who can still find no room for Jesus.

 # CONTEMPLATIO:

Spend a few minutes considering the four titles given to our Saviour in Isaiah 9:6: 'Wonderful Counsellor', 'Mighty God', 'Eternal Father', 'Prince of Peace'.

Reflect too on the message of Titus 2:11-14, that by God's grace we can live a life pleasing to God and look forward to the day when Jesus will return to earth again.

IN FATHER'S HOUSE

Luke 2:41-52

⁴¹ Every year the parents of Jesus went to Jerusalem for the Passover Festival. ⁴² When Jesus was twelve years old, they went to the festival as usual. ⁴³ When the festival was over, they started back home, but the boy Jesus stayed in Jerusalem. His parents did not know this; ⁴⁴ they thought that he was with the group, so they travelled a whole day and then started looking for him among their relatives and friends. ⁴⁵ They did not find him, so they went back to Jerusalem looking for him. ⁴⁶ On the third day they found him in the Temple, sitting with the Jewish teachers, listening to them and asking questions. ⁴⁷ All who heard him were amazed at his intelligent answers. ⁴⁸ His parents were astonished when they saw him, and his mother said to him, "My son, why have you done this to us? Your father and I have been terribly worried trying to find you."

⁴⁹ He answered them, "Why did you have to look for me? Didn't you know that I had to be in my Father's house?" ⁵⁰ But they did not understand his answer.

⁵¹ So Jesus went back with them to Nazareth, where he was obedient to them. His mother treasured all these things in her heart. ⁵² Jesus grew both in body and in wisdom, gaining favour with God and people.

Other Readings: 1 Samuel 1:20-22, 24-28; Psalm 84:1-2, 4-5, 8-9; 1 John 3:1-2, 21-24

 LECTIO:

After the events surrounding Jesus' miraculous birth we are given very few details about his childhood. This passage in Luke and another recorded in Matthew 2 (which we will read next Sunday) are the only two glimpses we are given.

As pious Jews, Mary and Joseph along with their relatives and friends, make their annual pilgrimage to Jerusalem. The occasion is the week-long Passover festival honouring God for saving and delivering their forefathers from Egypt (Exodus 12:1-27).

It was a trip they had made many times before. This year, however, proved to be particularly memorable. Instead of returning with everyone else Jesus, who at the age of twelve was probably on his first pilgrimage, remained behind in the temple.

When Joseph and Mary realise Jesus is not with their group they return to Jerusalem. After three anxious days searching they finally find him talking to the religious teachers in the temple!

Jesus appears to have been completely absorbed, spending four days at the temple. He was in his element; listening to the religious teachers and asking them questions. What stunned his listeners was his wisdom and understanding, far beyond his age and learning. There was clearly something special about this boy. It was a prophetic sign, giving a glimpse of who Jesus really is.

Mary and Joseph are understandably upset that Jesus didn't return home with them after the festival and caused them all this worry. Jesus' reply indicates that he took it for granted they would know where to find him; in the temple – 'in my Father's house'.

Mary and Joseph plainly didn't understand Jesus' words or actions although Mary 'treasured all these things in her heart'. After this event Luke tells us Jesus returned with them to Nazareth and was obedient to them. He grew up, increased in wisdom and gained favour with both God and man.

 MEDITATIO:

- What does this passage reveal to us about the twelve-year-old Jesus' thoughts regarding himself and his heavenly father?
- What does this passage tell us about Jesus' priorities? How would this be reflected in his future ministry?
- Jesus could have experienced God's presence anywhere. Why do you think he chose to go to the temple on this occasion?

 ORATIO:

We might capture something of Jesus' joy at being in his Father's house by praying the words of Psalm 84:2-9.

Today's passage focuses on family relationships with both our heavenly Father and our human family. Give thanks to God that you too are his child. Take time to pray for members of your church and of your own family.

 CONTEMPLATIO:

The verses in 1 John 3:1-2, 21-24 contain some amazing truths. Allow the wonder of a loving God who calls you his child to fill you.

Consider God's promise that we can live in union with him if we obey him.

THE NEW KING REVEALED

Matthew 2:1-12

¹ Jesus was born in the town of Bethlehem in Judea, during the time when Herod was king. Soon afterwards, some men who studied the stars came from the east to Jerusalem ² and asked, "Where is the baby born to be the king of the Jews? We saw his star when it came up in the east, and we have come to worship him."

³ When King Herod heard about this, he was very upset, and so was everyone else in Jerusalem. ⁴ He called together all the chief priests and the teachers of the Law and asked them, "Where will the Messiah be born?"

⁵ "In the town of Bethlehem in Judea," they answered. "For this is what the prophet wrote:

⁶ 'Bethlehem in the land of Judah,
  you are by no means the least of the leading cities of Judah;
for from you will come a leader
  who will guide my people Israel.' "

⁷ So Herod called the visitors from the east to a secret meeting and found out from them the exact time the star had appeared. ⁸ Then he sent them to Bethlehem with these instructions: "Go and make a careful search for the child, and when you find him, let me know, so that I too may go and worship him."

⁹ And so they left, and on their way they saw the same star they had seen in the east. When they saw it, how happy they were, what joy was theirs! It went ahead of them until it stopped over the place where the child was. ¹¹ They went into the house, and when they saw the child with his mother Mary, they knelt down and worshipped him. They brought out their gifts of gold, frankincense, and myrrh, and presented them to him.

¹² Then they returned to their country by another road, since God had warned them in a dream not to go back to Herod.

Other Readings: Isaiah 60:1-6; Psalm 72:1-2, 7-8, 10-13; Ephesians 3:2-3, 5-6

 LECTIO:

Matthew's great objective is to highlight Jesus as the fulfilment of the Old Testament prophecies for a Messiah or saviour.

Matthew relates several stories about Jesus' early years. The visit of the magi is well known, but were there three wise men? The Bible doesn't actually tell us how many wise men came, just that three gifts are given.

What is the significance of the visit? Some scholars suggest that the fact that the wise men came from another country indicated the worldwide significance of Jesus' birth. He would be a Messiah not only for the Jews but for all nations.

Herod is not pleased to hear about the arrival of a Messiah who might one day take his throne. After some careful questioning he sends the wise men on their way. The questions were more about saving his kingship than helping them. It seems from his earliest days Jesus forced people to choose.

The wise men set off for Bethlehem. Much to their delight they see the star again, which guides them to Jesus. They worship the new king and present to him their special gifts. God warns them in a dream not to reveal Jesus' identity to Herod. So having fulfilled their mission they return home via another route.

 MEDITATIO:

- Consider why God chose people from another country to reveal the birth of the Messiah to King Herod.
- The wise men's visit alerted Herod and the people of Jerusalem to the Messiah's birth. But they are only given part of the picture at this point. Consider God's purposes in this.
- Think about the different ways we can worship Jesus. What 'gifts' could you offer him today?
- Who is Jesus to you: a king or your King? What practical difference does your answer make to the way you live?

 ORATIO:

Psalm 72 was written for the coronation of a king; down the ages it has often been interpreted as referring to the Messiah. Pray through the verses selected for today.

Pray for leaders, governments and people in authority to rule and act justly. Ask God to help those who have been treated unfairly.

 CONTEMPLATIO:

The wise men worshipped Jesus as a great King even though they only saw him as a baby. Spend some time in adoration of the true King of Kings.

HEAVEN OPENED

Luke 3:15-16, 21-22

[15] People's hopes began to rise, and they began to wonder whether John perhaps might be the Messiah. [16] So John said to all of them, "I baptize you with water, but someone is coming who is much greater than I am. I am not good enough even to untie his sandals. He will baptize you with the Holy Spirit and fire.

[21] After all the people had been baptized, Jesus also was baptized. While he was praying, heaven was opened, [22] and the Holy Spirit came down upon him in bodily form like a dove. And a voice came from heaven, "You are my own dear Son. I am pleased with you."

Other Readings: Isaiah 40:1-5, 9-11; Psalm 104:1-4, 24-25, 27-30; Titus 2:11-14, 3:4-7

 LECTIO:

Luke is our guide through this event which launches Jesus into his salvation ministry. Luke reminds us of the Jewish nation's huge anticipation of a Messiah, or Saviour. The Messiah was well known to them in some respects, all the great prophets spoke of his coming. And yet the people were still waiting.

Over the years, especially in unsettled times, people must have looked carefully at many notable people. Now they wondered, even hoped, that John might be the promised Messiah. John swiftly dashed those hopes and proclaimed the imminent arrival of the real Saviour, who 'will baptize you with the Holy Spirit and fire'.

John revealed the Saviour was to be a spiritual not political leader. He would baptize people with the Holy Spirit. It was a rather obscure promise to make - how would John's followers respond? Would they understand?

Here beside the river Jordan Jesus is baptized along with everyone else. Although he had not sinned he is nonetheless willing to identify with ordinary sinful people in a public act of repentance and conversion.

Matthew records John's shocked reaction when Jesus steps up for baptism (Matthew 3:13-15). But Luke focuses on Jesus and the Holy Spirit.

Jesus remains in prayer and contemplation after his baptism. Then the miracle occurs, Jesus sees the Holy Spirit descend on him in the form of a dove. And Jesus' prayer becomes a communion, as the Father speaks to him and affirms him.

One thing we can note is that as soon as Jesus has identified with humankind, in the baptism of repentance, his Father speaks out loud and clear, "You are my own dear Son. I am pleased with you.".

 MEDITATIO:

- What made John appear to be the promised Messiah? And why was John's baptism necessary? How could it help the people prepare for Jesus and his message?
- The baptism of Jesus became an 'epiphany', a revelation of God – in the form of Father, Son, and Holy Spirit (the dove). What might this experience and manifestation have meant for Jesus himself?
- Imagine you were there and saw the dove and heard God's voice. How would this influence your opinion of Jesus?

 ORATIO:

Psalm 104 is a vibrant song of praise. The opening verse declares:
    'Praise the Lord, my soul!
    O Lord, my God, how great you are!'
In the following thirty-four verses the psalmist looks at the everyday world around him and sees God's hand in it all. Praise just bubbles up and pours out to God.

Read through the verses slowly. Then write your own list of reasons to praise God and offer this to him as a prayer of worship. You may want to make this into your very own psalm to God.

 CONTEMPLATIO:

Consider today's verses from Isaiah and what they reveal about both Jesus and John the Baptist. Let the promises contained in these few verses sink deep into your heart.

Think about the great words of St Paul in his letter to Titus. Our salvation is based upon God's mercy and he gives us the grace to live our lives in a way that pleases him.

God wants us to have eternal life with him and has done everything to make it possible. Another wonderful promise full of hope that we should allow to settle in our hearts.

WEDDING MIRACLE

John 2:1-11

[1] Two days later there was a wedding in the town of Cana in Galilee. Jesus' mother was there, [2] and Jesus and his disciples had also been invited to the wedding. [3] When the wine had given out, Jesus' mother said to him, "They have no wine left."

[4] "You must not tell me what to do," Jesus replied. "My time has not yet come."

[5] Jesus' mother then told the servants, "Do whatever he tells you."

[6] The Jews have rules about ritual washing, and for this purpose six stone water jars were there, each one large enough to hold about a hundred litres. [7] Jesus said to the servants, "Fill these jars with water." They filled them to the brim, [8] and then he told them, "Now draw some water out and take it to the man in charge of the feast." They took him the water, [9] which now had turned into wine, and he tasted it. He did not know where this wine had come from (but, of course, the servants who had drawn out the water knew); so he called the bridegroom [10] and said to him, "Everyone else serves the best wine first, and after the guests have had plenty to drink, he serves the ordinary wine. But you have kept the best wine until now!"

[11] Jesus performed this first miracle in Cana in Galilee; there he revealed his glory, and his disciples believed in him.

Other Readings: Isaiah 62:1-5; Psalm 96:1-3, 7-10; 1 Corinthians 12:4-11

 LECTIO:

John often tells us about events not related in the other Gospels. The wedding at Cana is one of them.

Much of the focus in this passage is on Jesus and his mother Mary. Many details are not included, so as we read the passage the questions start to pop up. How did Jesus come to know the bride and groom? Did Jesus know their families? Were the bride and groom followers of Jesus? Were all the disciples there?

John turns our attention to the wine running out. This would have been a major disgrace for the bride's family and would have spoilt the bride and groom's special day.

Only a few short words are exchanged between Jesus and Mary. Have they had conversations like this before about Jesus' ministry? We are not told.

When Mary speaks about the need for wine, Jesus takes this to mean she is asking him to do something about it. But he is reluctant. Mary doesn't give up hope. She simply tells the servants to do whatever Jesus tells them. Mary doesn't ask for a miracle in so many words but perhaps this is what she is hoping for.

Jesus instructs the servants to fill six huge stone jars with water. The servants follow Jesus' instructions and the water miraculously becomes wine.

We are not specifically told whether the wedding guests know about this miracle at the time. But surely the servants would have talked about this amazing event - if not during the wedding itself then afterwards.

We are however told that the disciples did know about it and this miracle caused them to believe in Jesus. John also adds the interesting detail that the wine Jesus produced was no ordinary wine – it was top quality!

 ## MEDITATIO:

- Meditate on the symbolism in this miracle – the bride and groom, a wedding celebration, the new wine.
- How surprised are you that Jesus' first miracle is turning water into wine? Why do you think Jesus went ahead and performed the miracle?
- What does this passage reveal about what Mary believed about her son?

 ## ORATIO:

Psalm 96 is a wonderful song of praise. Why not join the psalmist and make his words part of your daily prayer this week,

'Proclaim every day the good news that he has saved us.'

 ## CONTEMPLATIO:

Allow God to cherish you and lavish the gifts of his Spirit on you. We are part of the church, which the Bible tells us is the bride of Jesus himself. It is his great pleasure to lavish his love on his bride.

As God's love flows over you remember God's desire to have a perfect bride. Don't lose heart. God can transform his bride as easily and wonderfully as Jesus transformed the wine.

LIBERTY PROCLAIMED

Luke 1:1-4, 4:14-21

Luke 1

¹ Dear Theophilus:

Many people have done their best to write a report of the things that have taken place among us. ² They wrote what we have been told by those who saw these things from the beginning and who proclaimed the message. ³ And so, your Excellency, because I have carefully studied all these matters from their beginning, I thought it would be good to write an orderly account for you. ⁴ I do this so that you will know the full truth about everything which you have been taught.

Luke 4

¹⁴ Then Jesus returned to Galilee, and the power of the Holy Spirit was with him. The news about him spread throughout all that territory. ¹⁵ He taught in the synagogues and was praised by everyone.

¹⁶ Then Jesus went to Nazareth, where he had been brought up, and on the Sabbath he went as usual to the synagogue. He stood up to read the Scriptures ¹⁷ and was handed the book of the prophet Isaiah. He unrolled the scroll and found the place where it is written:

¹⁸ "The Spirit of the Lord is upon me,

because he has chosen me to bring good news to the poor.

He has sent me to proclaim liberty to the captives

and recovery of sight to the blind;

to set free the oppressed

¹⁹ and announce that the time has come

when the Lord will save his people."

²⁰ Jesus rolled up the scroll, gave it back to the attendant, and sat down. All the people in the synagogue had their eyes fixed on him, ²¹ as he said to them, "This passage of scripture has come true today, as you heard it being read."

Other Readings: Nehemiah 8:2-6, 8-10; Psalm 19:7-9, 14; 1 Corinthians 12:12-30

 # LECTIO:

Two extracts from the Gospel of Luke are presented together today. The first is an introduction to the second.

In Chapter 1 Luke is keen to show the quality and reliability of his information. Firstly he has spoken to eye witnesses of the events he describes, and secondly he has done extensive research. So his report is not the sort of 'embroidered news' you can hear in the market or read in newspapers. The letter is addressed to Theophilus, which means 'God's friend'.

Jesus' visit to the synagogue in Nazareth is the focus of Chapter 4. While Isaiah is chosen for him, it appears Jesus selects these specific verses. He reads them to the gathered community.

Jesus then teaches on the meaning of these words. He tells them that Isaiah's prophecy, written hundreds of years ago, 'has come true today'! The implication is that Jesus himself is the fulfilment of these words. Local man Jesus now comes with the good news for the poor, freedom to captives, sight to the blind, and freedom to the oppressed. We are not told whether Jesus is speaking literally or metaphorically here.

But how did this community feel when Jesus spoke out that Sabbath morning? What happened in their hearts and minds? Did Jesus' words make any sense?

While this event took place two thousand years ago the truth of God's Word is everlasting. So reading of Scripture should never be just a mere cultural event. Whenever the Scriptures are proclaimed they are alive, active and always full of power.

 # MEDITATIO:

- What do you think the people listening to Jesus would have understood when he said, 'This passage of scripture has come true today, as you heard it being read.'?
- How well do you think these verses from Isaiah sum up Jesus' ministry on earth? In what ways did Jesus fulfil this prophecy?
- Consider the good news of the Gospel. Give thanks for all the ways it is true for you personally.

 # ORATIO:

Pray that in your church everyone will play their part so the whole church functions healthily, as Paul describes in 1 Corinthians 12: 12-30.

Pray about your role in this. Ask God to show you if there are things you should be doing or allowing others to do.

 # CONTEMPLATIO:

Reflect on Nehemiah 8:10:
'The joy that the Lord gives you will make you strong.'

FAITH REQUIRED

Luke 4:21-30

²¹ as he said to them, "This passage of scripture has come true today, as you heard it being read."

²² They were all well impressed with him and marvelled at the eloquent words that he spoke. They said, "Isn't he the son of Joseph?"

²³ He said to them, "I am sure that you will quote this proverb to me, 'Doctor, heal yourself.' You will also tell me to do here in my home town the same things you heard were done in Capernaum. ²⁴ I tell you this," Jesus added, "prophets are never welcomed in their home town.

²⁵ "Listen to me: it is true that there were many widows in Israel during the time of Elijah, when there was no rain for three and a half years and a severe famine spread throughout the whole land. ²⁶ Yet Elijah was not sent to anyone in Israel, but only to a widow living in Zarephath in the territory of Sidon. ²⁷ And there were many people suffering from a dreaded skin disease who lived in Israel during the time of the prophet Elisha; yet not one of them was healed, but only Naaman the Syrian."

²⁸ When the people in the synagogue heard this, they were filled with anger. ²⁹ They rose up, dragged Jesus out of the town, and took him to the top of the hill on which their town was built. They meant to throw him over the cliff, ³⁰ but he walked through the middle of the crowd and went his way.

Other Readings: Jeremiah 1:4-5, 17-19; Psalm 71:1-6, 15, 17;
1 Corinthians 12:31-13:13

 LECTIO:

This week's reading continues the passage we started last week. We are still in the synagogue in Nazareth but the atmosphere changes dramatically. From being impressed with his eloquent words (verse 22) the congregation become angry, drag Jesus out of town and want to throw him over a cliff (verse 28-29).

While there was amazement at Jesus' teaching and his remarkable claim to be the fulfilment of Isaiah's prophecy – the Messiah – there was no faith or acceptance in the people. They simply could not accept a carpenter's son and the Messiah as one and the same person.

Jesus reminded them of how it was for Elijah and Elisha. These great prophets also suffered disbelief from their own people.

Elijah was the first great prophet God used to call his people back to him. Elijah prophesied a drought to King Ahab. When the three-year drought began God used a raven, an unclean bird, and a foreigner to save Elijah. The Lebanese woman took Elijah at his word and through her God saved the prophet. No Israelite helped him.

Elisha, Elijah's successor as a prophet, healed Naaman, a Syrian army general, from a dreaded skin disease. Naaman did what Elisha asked him to do even though he thought it was foolish. He was completely healed and believed.

Not surprisingly Jesus' words angered the people of Nazareth. They deeply resented the comparison with the faithless Israelites of Elijah and Elisha's time. So they decided to get rid of the problem by killing Jesus.

The people in the synagogue were religious Sabbath-observing Jews. But they were not people of faith and so they rejected Jesus. They only saw the 'local boy', not the Saviour of mankind, and threw away the chance to become his disciples.

 MEDITATIO:

- What can we learn from this passage about the sort of faith Jesus is looking for? Just attending church and listening to the sermon without faith isn't enough.
- What can we learn from the two examples Jesus gives of the widow and Naaman? You can read these stories in 1 Kings 17:8-16 and 2 Kings 5:1-14.
- What can help our faith grow? How can we put the sort of faith Jesus seeks into action?

 ORATIO:

Pray through the verses selected from Psalm 71. Ask God for opportunities to tell others how wonderful he is and how he has helped you.

 CONTEMPLATIO:

Read 1 Corinthians 12:31-13:13 through several times. As you sit with God allow him to reveal gently where he might want you to grow: in faith, or hope or love.

Consider God's amazing words to the prophet in Jeremiah 1:4-5, 17-19. Which words strike you? What might God be saying to you?

FISHERS OF MEN

Luke 5:1-11

¹ One day Jesus was standing on the shore of Lake Gennesaret while the people pushed their way up to him to listen to the word of God. ² He saw two boats pulled up on the beach; the fishermen had left them and were washing the nets. ³ Jesus got into one of the boats – it belonged to Simon – and asked him to push off a little from the shore. Jesus sat in the boat and taught the crowd.

⁴ When he finished speaking, he said to Simon, "Push the boat out further to the deep water, and you and your partners let down your nets for a catch."

⁵ "Master," Simon answered, "we worked hard all night long and caught nothing. But if you say so, I will let down the nets." ⁶ They let them down and caught such a large number of fish that the nets were about to break. ⁷ So they motioned to their partners in the other boat to come and help them. They came and filled both boats so full of fish that the boats were about to sink. ⁸ When Simon Peter saw what had happened, he fell on his knees before Jesus and said, "Go away from me, Lord! I am a sinful man!"

⁹ He and the others with him were all amazed at the large number of fish they had caught. ¹⁰ The same was true of Simon's partners, James and John, the sons of Zebedee. Jesus said to Simon, "Don't be afraid; from now on you will be catching people."

¹¹ They pulled the boats up on the beach, left everything, and followed Jesus.

Other Readings: Isaiah 6:1-8; Psalm 138: 1-5, 7-8; 1 Corinthians 15:1-11

 LECTIO:

This is such a well known story that we can read it and yet not get to the heart of this miraculous event. Luke invites us to become witnesses to the miracle and of the call of the first three disciples into service.

Crowds were already following Jesus to listen to him teaching on the word of God. What did they see in Jesus – was it something more than a simple preacher? Or did they recognise God's representative?

When Simon witnesses the miraculous catch of fish he sees Jesus in a new light. He acknowledges Jesus as 'Lord' (verse 8) and feels the burden of his sinfulness before Jesus. He immediately falls to his knees and asks Jesus to leave him. The prophet Isaiah reacted in a similar way when he saw a vision of God (see Isaiah 6).

God seems to give both men impossible missions. Jesus tells Simon not to be afraid and then tells him he has a new job – catching people, not fish! We are not given any more details at this stage but Luke hints it is Jesus who will turn these humble fishermen into 'catchers of people'.

Simon and the other new disciples are captivated by Jesus and leave with him. Implicit in what Jesus has said is the need for the disciples to be with Jesus all the time to fulfil their vocation. Nets, boats, livelihood, homes and families are all left behind as the disciples set off with Jesus for a totally new life.

MEDITATIO:

- What does Simon's initial reaction to this miracle reveal about who he thought Jesus was?
- Have you ever experienced the burden of your sinfulness? How do you think God wants us to respond to him at this time? What can we learn from Simon's response?
- To become a 'catcher of people' Simon, James and John had to spend time with Jesus and follow him. What does this mean for us today? Is every Christian called to be 'a catcher of people'? If so how can we draw practical lessons from Jesus in the time we spend with him?

ORATIO:

Give thanks that we can know forgiveness of our sins because of Jesus' death and resurrection. 1 John 1:9 gives us the assurance that 'if we confess our sins to God... he will forgive us our sins and purify us from all our wrongdoing.'

Ask God to help you forget your own frailties and to give you the faith and courage to follow Jesus and tell others about him.

CONTEMPLATIO:

Contemplate God's pure holiness. Join the seraphim in declaring God's holiness and glory.

RIGHT PRIORITIES

Luke 6:17, 20-26

¹⁷ When Jesus had come down from the hill with the apostles, he stood on a level place with a large number of his disciples. A large crowd of people was there from all over Judea and from Jerusalem and from the coastal cities of Tyre and Sidon;

²⁰ Jesus looked at his disciples and said,

"Happy are you poor;
     the Kingdom of God is yours!
²¹ Happy are you who are hungry now;
     you will be filled!
Happy are you who weep now;
     you will laugh!

²² "Happy are you when people hate you, reject you, insult you, and say that you are evil, all because of the Son of Man! ²³ Be glad when that happens, and dance for joy, because a great reward is kept for you in heaven. For their ancestors did the very same things to the prophets.

²⁴ "But how terrible for you who are rich now;
     you have had your easy life!
²⁵ How terrible for you who are full now;
     you will go hungry!
How terrible for you who laugh now;
     you will mourn and weep!

²⁶ "How terrible when all people speak well of you; their ancestors said the very same things about the false prophets.

Other Readings: Jeremiah 17:5-8; Psalm 1:1-4, 6; 1 Corinthians 15:12, 16-20

 LECTIO:

Both Matthew and Luke's gospels record an account of Jesus' ethical teaching. There are quite a few differences between the two reports. Matthew gives Jesus' teaching on 'real happiness' in nine statements – the Beatitudes (Matthew 5:3-12).

Luke uses the technique of contrast to emphasise the points and reduces the number of different situations that Jesus says bring blessing from nine to four.

Now to the heart of Jesus' teaching. Jesus teaches that the four situations of poverty, hunger, weeping and rejection because of him become sources of blessing. Jesus gives a completely new perspective on life and offers hope and comfort to everyone in these circumstances. Our human nature is to try and avoid these things but Jesus warns that it is their opposites – wealth, gluttony, gloating and a 'good' reputation – that can be our ruin.

Perhaps the truth is written so clearly we can't see it. These four times of difficulty can bring us into total dependence on God where our focus is completely on him. But in times of plenty it is much too easy to see ourselves and our possessions as the source of our happiness instead of pleasing God. Jesus knows otherwise and wants us to grasp the fact that God himself is our only guarantee of happiness and security.

 # MEDITATIO:

- What do you think about Jesus' teaching in these verses? What strikes you most?
- Consider Matthew 6:33 '...be concerned above everything else with the Kingdom of God and what he requires of you...' How can we ensure that, whatever our circumstances, our top priority is always serving God and doing what he tells us to do?
- Think about the image of a tree planted by water in Jeremiah 17 and Psalm 1. In what ways are you putting your roots down deep into God?

 # ORATIO:

Pray the words of today's responsorial verse 'Happy are those who trust the Lord...' (Psalm 40:4) Ask the Holy Spirit to gently reveal any areas of your life where you need to trust God more or change your priorities.

To build up your own trust try keeping a prayer notebook. Jot down your prayers each day. And then take a few minutes each week to add a comment beside each prayer as you see them answered. This is a real faith and trust builder.

 # CONTEMPLATIO:

Consider the example we have in Jesus. He single-mindedly listened to his Father and followed his plan.

Think about some of the ways God demonstrated his faithfulness to people in the Bible. Now think about the times God has been faithful to you personally.

OVERCOMING TEMPTATION

Luke 4:1-13

¹ Jesus returned from the Jordan full of the Holy Spirit and was led by the Spirit into the desert, ² where he was tempted by the Devil for 40 days. In all that time he ate nothing, so that he was hungry when it was over.

³ The Devil said to him, "If you are God's Son, order this stone to turn into bread."

⁴ But Jesus answered, "The scripture says, 'Human beings cannot live on bread alone.'

⁵ Then the Devil took him up and showed him in a second all the kingdoms of the world. ⁶ "I will give you all this power and all this wealth," the Devil told him. "It has all been handed over to me, and I can give it to anyone I choose. ⁷ All this will be yours, then, if you worship me."

⁸ Jesus answered, "The scripture says, 'Worship the Lord your God and serve only him!'"

⁹ Then the Devil took him to Jerusalem and set him on the highest point of the Temple, and said to him, "If you are God's Son, throw yourself down from here. ¹⁰ For the scripture says, 'God will order his angels to take good care of you.' ¹¹ It also says, 'They will hold you up with their hands so that not even your feet will be hurt on the stones.'"

¹² But Jesus answered, "The scripture says, 'Do not put the Lord your God to the test.'"

¹³ When the Devil finished tempting Jesus in every way, he left him for a while.

Other Readings: Deuteronomy 26:4-10; Psalm 91:1-2, 10-15; Romans 10:8-13

 LECTIO:

Jesus on his divine mission is led by the Holy Spirit into the desert. He stays there for forty days and fasts the whole time. Forty is significant as a time of preparation in the Old Testament. It recalls Moses fasting forty days on Mount Sinai (Exodus 34:28) and the Israelites spending forty years in the wilderness before entering the Promised Land (Deuteronomy 8:2-3, 29:5-6).

We only hear about three specific temptations, but it is clear that this was not the only time Jesus was tempted: the Devil left him 'for a while' (verse 13).

The Devil tempts Jesus to use his supernatural power to meet his own physical need. Jesus rejects this misuse of his power. He identifies with you and me. We need more than just physical food. The implication is clear that we also need 'spiritual food' from God.

The Devil then offers to hand over power over the nations if Jesus will worship him. Jesus had indeed come to save people from the Devil's control, but not this way.

Lastly the Devil tempts Jesus to prove his divine nature by throwing himself off the temple so God will send his angels to rescue him.

These three temptations illustrate the core of every temptation: the desire to push God aside, to regard him secondary and redundant, to rely solely on one's own strength, and to put the world right without God.

Jesus is not deceived by the Devil's cunning deceptions even when he uses scripture itself to tempt him. Jesus rebuts every temptation with scripture, quoting successively from Deuteronomy 8:3, 6:13 and 6:16. Authentic interpretation of a portion of scripture must be consistent with the whole of scripture.

For Jesus and for us, the essence of all temptation is to be offered an appealing alternative to God's way of doing things rather than obeying him.

 # MEDITATIO:

- What helped Jesus reject these temptations? What lessons can we learn to help us overcome the temptations we face? Consider what 'spiritual food' will help us stay close to God.
- Jesus was single-minded about doing things God's way. He avoided being deceived into doing anything else. How can we try to follow his example?
- Consider this verse from Hebrews 4:15. What encouragement does it offer us?
  'Our High Priest is not one who cannot feel sympathy for our weaknesses. On the contrary, we have a High Priest who was tempted in every way that we are, but did not sin.'

 # ORATIO:

The Lord's prayer (Matthew 6:9-13) reminds us to pray about temptation. Throughout the week ask God to deliver you from the things that tempt you.

Use the words from Psalm 91 to inspire your prayers today.

 # CONTEMPLATIO:

Spend some time treasuring the promises in Romans 10:9-11:
  'If you confess that Jesus is Lord and believe that God raised him from death, you will be saved.' (v.9)
  'Whoever believes in him will not be disappointed.' (v.11)

GOD'S CHOSEN ONE

Luke 9:28-36

²⁸ About a week after he had said these things, Jesus took Peter, John, and James with him and went up a hill to pray. ²⁹ While he was praying, his face changed its appearance, and his clothes became dazzling white. ³⁰ Suddenly two men were there talking with him. They were Moses and Elijah, ³¹ who appeared in heavenly glory and talked with Jesus about the way in which he would soon fulfil God's purpose by dying in Jerusalem. ³² Peter and his companions were sound asleep, but they woke up and saw Jesus' glory and the two men who were standing with him. ³³ As the men were leaving Jesus, Peter said to him, "Master, how good it is that we are here! We will make three tents, one for you, one for Moses, and one for Elijah." (He did not really know what he was saying.)

³⁴ While he was still speaking, a cloud appeared and covered them with its shadow; and the disciples were afraid as the cloud came over them. ³⁵ A voice said from the cloud, "This is my Son, whom I have chosen – listen to him!"

³⁶ When the voice stopped, there was Jesus all alone. The disciples kept quiet about all this, and told no one at that time anything they had seen.

Other Readings: Genesis 15:5-12, 17-18; Psalm 27:1, 7-9, 13-14; Philippians 3:17-4:1

 LECTIO:

Jesus chooses only his first three disciples – Peter, John and James - to climb a mountain with him for a prayer time. We don't know how long Jesus prays but the disciples fall asleep. It appears that the disciples wake up just in time to witness the end of a remarkable encounter. Jesus' clothes are now dazzling white and he is talking to Moses and Elijah.

The appearance of Moses and Elijah is significant. Moses led the exodus of God's people out of slavery in Egypt and many Jews expected the prophet Elijah to return before the coming of the Messiah. They talk with Jesus about how he will soon fulfil God's purpose through his death (or 'exodus', the literal meaning of Luke's writing here) in Jerusalem. God's salvation plan for mankind, bringing true and lasting deliverance, is being fulfilled in Jesus.

This experience may have strengthened Jesus for the testing days ahead that would culminate with his death on the cross. Luke makes no comment on this. What is clear is that God is present, as indicated by the cloud which veils his glory. As at Jesus' baptism, God speaks. He affirms Jesus as his Son whom he has chosen. And this time God adds the instruction to the disciples to 'listen to him'.

This event, together with the other miracles and teaching that surround it, gave the disciples glimpses of who Jesus was. But they needed to travel much further with Jesus. In fact they needed to meet him after the resurrection to really understand who he was and his mission on earth.

 # MEDITATIO:

- Imagine you were one of the disciples that witnessed this event. How might you have felt? What would you have learnt?
- What has Jesus been chosen for? In what way does his death in Jerusalem fulfil God's purpose?
- In what ways can we 'listen to him' as God told the disciples to do?
- What is your experience of prayer? Do you find it as easy to listen to God as to talk to him?

 # ORATIO:

Thank God for the words from today's responsorial Psalm:

'The Lord is my light and my salvation;'

Thank God each day this week for all the ways he has guided and saved you. Ask him to deepen your appreciation of his salvation for you.

Ask the Holy Spirit to overshadow you, to transform your life so that people around you notice something different about the way you live. Ask God to help you reflect more of Jesus to others.

 # CONTEMPLATIO:

Consider the glory of Jesus' transfigured body. For Christians, Paul offers us a tremendous promise, 'He will change our weak mortal bodies and make them like his own glorious body...' (Philippians 3:21).

Consider what it means that we are now 'citizens of heaven' (Philippians 3:20).

REPENT AND BELIEVE

Luke 13:1-9

[1] At that time some people were there who told Jesus about the Galileans whom Pilate had killed while they were offering sacrifices to God. [2] Jesus answered them, "Because those Galileans were killed in that way, do you think it proves that they were worse sinners than all the other Galileans? [3] No indeed! And I tell you that if you do not turn from your sins, you will all die as they did. [4] What about those eighteen people in Siloam who were killed when the tower fell on them? Do you suppose this proves that they were worse than all the other people living in Jerusalem? [5] No indeed! And I tell you that if you do not turn from your sins, you will all die as they did."

[6] Then Jesus told them this parable: "There was once a man who had a fig tree growing in his vineyard. He went looking for figs on it but found none. [7] So he said to his gardener, 'Look, for three years I have been coming here looking for figs on this fig tree, and I haven't found any. Cut it down! Why should it go on using up the soil?' [8] But the gardener answered, 'Leave it alone, sir, just one more year; I will dig round it and put in some manure. [9] Then if the tree bears figs next year, so much the better; if not, then you can have it cut down.'"

Other Readings: Exodus 3:1-8, 13-15; Psalm 103:1-4, 6-8, 11;
1 Corinthians 10:1-6, 10-12

 LECTIO:

Luke reveals Jesus using current events to teach important lessons. The two events are quite different; one was political, the other an accident, but in both cases many people died.

In the first event, Pilate shockingly had some Galileans murdered even while they were offering their sacrifices to God. Their lives were suddenly cut short at the very time they performed the most sacred of religious acts in the holiest place, the temple.

We don't know why Pilate chose to have people killed in the temple. People thought that these Galileans must have been really bad to be killed in this way. They speculated that God took no pleasure in their sacrifices and so allowed this sacrilege to occur.

Then Jesus considers a second event, this time a complete accident, when a tower collapsed killing eighteen people.

Jesus makes it clear that in both cases the people that died were no worse than his listeners or anyone else. He insists we must all repent and turn away from our sins otherwise we will be judged and punished by God.

Jesus develops his teaching by telling a parable about a fig-less fig tree. The tree has not produced any figs for three years and is in danger of being cut down. The gardener asks for one more year so he can give it special attention to help it produce fruit. But if the tree remained barren after all the extra care it would be removed.

Jesus warns his listeners not to be like the fig tree. Changed lives bear kingdom fruit and his teaching was an opportunity for them to consider their lives, repent and turn to God.

 # MEDITATIO:

- What does this passage have to say about thinking we are better than others? Whose standard is the one that counts?
- Do you see any link between Jesus and the gardener who begged for the chance to care for the fig tree and save it from being destroyed?
- What do you think the figs might represent in this parable?
- Consider what the passage tells us about God's character – his patience, mercy and holiness.

 # ORATIO:

Use the verses from Psalm 103 for a time of fellowship and prayer with God. Remember his love, mercy and kindness. Worship him for his holiness. Thank him that he forgives our sins – even though we don't deserve it.

Ask him how your life could be more fruitful for him.

 # CONTEMPLATIO:

Jesus' death on the cross opened a door into God's presence (Hebrews 4:14-16). Now we can come before God's throne at any time. Sit or kneel in God's presence for a while and consider his pure holiness.

LOST AND FOUND

Luke 15:1-3, 11-32

[1] One day when many tax collectors and other outcasts came to listen to Jesus, [2] the Pharisees and the teachers of the Law started grumbling, "This man welcomes outcasts and even eats with them!" [3] So Jesus told them this parable:

[11] Jesus went on to say, "There was once a man who had two sons. [12] The younger one said to him, 'Father, give me my share of the property now.' So the man divided his property between his two sons. [13] After a few days the younger son sold his part of the property and left home with the money. He went to a country far away, where he wasted his money in reckless living. [14] He spent everything he had. Then a severe famine spread over that country, and he was left without a thing. [15] So he went to work for one of the citizens of that country, who sent him out to his farm to take care of the pigs. [16] He wished he could fill himself with the bean pods the pigs ate, but no one gave him anything to eat. [17] At last he came to his senses and said, 'All my father's hired workers have more than they can eat, and here I am about to starve! [18] I will get up and go to my father and say, Father, I have sinned against God and against you. [19] I am no longer fit to be called your son; treat me as one of your hired workers.' [20] So he got up and started back to his father.

"He was still a long way from home when his father saw him; his heart was filled with pity, and he ran, threw his arms round his son, and kissed him. [21] 'Father,' the son said, 'I have sinned against God and against you. I am no longer fit to be called your son.' [22] But the father called his servants. 'Hurry!' he said. 'Bring the best robe and put it on him. Put a ring on his finger and shoes on his feet. [23] Then go and get the prize calf and kill it, and let us celebrate with a feast! [24] For this son of mine was dead, but now he is alive; he was lost, but now he has been found.' And so the feasting began.

[25] "In the meantime the elder son was out in the field. On his way back, when he came close to the house, he heard the music and dancing. [26] So he called one of the servants and asked him, 'What's going on?' [27] 'Your brother has come back home,' the servant answered, 'and your father has killed the prize calf, because he got him back safe and sound.'

[28] "The elder brother was so angry that he would not go into the house; so his father came out and begged him to come in. [29] But he answered his father, 'Look, all these years I have worked for you like a slave, and I have never disobeyed your orders. What have you given me? Not even a goat for me to have a feast with my friends! [30] But this son of yours wasted all your property on prostitutes, and when he comes back home, you kill the prize calf for him!' [31] 'My son,' the father

answered, 'you are always here with me, and everything I have is yours. [32] But we had to celebrate and be happy, because your brother was dead, but now he is alive; he was lost, but now he has been found.' "

Other Readings: Joshua 5:9-12; Psalm 33:2-7; 2 Corinthians 5:17-21

 # LECTIO:

This parable is one of the best known illustrations of God's love and mercy. It shows Jesus' love for sinners is rooted in God the Father's love.

The story speeds through the younger son's squandering of his inheritance, humiliation, repentance and decision to risk returning home.

The father welcomes his son back with open arms and throws a feast to celebrate. Not so the older brother, who resents his father's lavish forgiveness.

 # MEDITATIO:

- Make a list of the different challenges the two sons faced.
- Which son do you identify with most? What does this passage have to say to you?
- What can we learn from the actions of the father?

 # ORATIO:

Prayerfully read 2 Corinthians 5:17-21. Ask the Holy Spirit what to pray and then respond to his leading.

 # CONTEMPLATIO:

Consider the father's great love for both his sons. Now think about God's love and mercy for you.

A LESSON IN MERCY

John 8:1-11

[1] Then everyone went home, but Jesus went to the Mount of Olives. [2] Early the next morning he went back to the Temple. All the people gathered round him, and he sat down and began to teach them. [3] The teachers of the Law and the Pharisees brought in a woman who had been caught committing adultery, and they made her stand before them all. [4] "Teacher," they said to Jesus, "this woman was caught in the very act of committing adultery. [5] In our Law Moses commanded that such a woman must be stoned to death. Now, what do you say?" [6] They said this to trap Jesus, so that they could accuse him. But he bent over and wrote on the ground with his finger.

[7] As they stood there asking him questions, he straightened himself up and said to them, "Whichever one of you has committed no sin may throw the first stone at her." [8] Then he bent over again and wrote on the ground. [9] When they heard this, they all left, one by one, the older ones first. Jesus was left alone, with the woman still standing there. [10] He straightened himself up and said to her, "Where are they? Is there no one left to condemn you?"

[11] "No one, sir," she answered.

"Well, then," Jesus said, "I do not condemn you either. Go, but do not sin again."

Other Readings: Isaiah 43:16-21; Psalm 126; Philippians 3:8-14

 LECTIO:

This week we read another example of Jesus' forgiveness and mercy. A woman has been caught in adultery. The Pharisees, knowing Jesus' compassion for sinners, take this opportunity to try and trap him.

Picture the scene. Jesus is teaching in the temple, the holiest place for the Jews which Jesus described as 'my Father's house'. A crowd of people are gathered around listening to what he has to say.

A group of Pharisees and teachers of the Law arrive and make a woman stand before Jesus and the crowd. They declare that she was caught in adultery and that the punishment required by the Law of Moses is death by stoning (Deuteronomy 22: 22-24). Then comes the loaded question, "Now, what do you say?" They pretend to accuse only the woman, but they are actually looking for a chance to accuse (and try) Jesus.

The man with whom she was committing adultery is not mentioned, nor is her husband. The atmosphere must have been electric. It was quite literally a matter of life and death. All eyes shift from the woman, whose life hangs in the balance, to Jesus. What will he say?

Jesus bends down and writes on the ground. What did he write? Why? Perhaps Jesus wanted to draw attention away from the terrified woman, perhaps he was considering his answer. John gives no explanation.

Jesus' answer is masterful. He is well aware of the intended trap. He silences the accusers without contradicting the Law or condoning the sin. The woman is eventually left on her own before Jesus. As he was without sin he could have carried out the punishment but he tells her she is free to go. He wants to give her the opportunity to repent and tells her not to sin again.

 MEDITATIO:

- Compare the way the Pharisees treated this woman with the way Jesus treated her. Consider their actions and motives. How did they differ? Were there any points of agreement?
- Imagine yourself firstly as one of the Pharisees, then as this frightened woman. What impact do you think this encounter would have had on you?
- What can we learn from this passage about our attitudes to our own behaviour and our attitudes to others?

 ORATIO:

Thank God for his grace and mercy. He knows our weaknesses and when we sin we can come to him to be forgiven and restored. Ask God to deepen your appreciation of these wonderfully undeserved gifts.

Pray through Psalm 126 and give thanks for 'What marvels the Lord has worked for us!'

Ask the Holy Spirit to reveal any attitudes in you that should change.

 CONTEMPLATIO:

Consider the images of water in Isaiah 43 and Psalm 126. Let God reveal its life-sustaining, refreshing and cleansing properties. Now relate this to God's forgiveness and grace in your life.

WELCOME THE KING

Luke 19:28-40

[28] After Jesus said this, he went on ahead of them to Jerusalem. [29] As he came near Bethphage and Bethany at the Mount of Olives, he sent two disciples ahead [30] with these instructions: "Go to the village there ahead of you; as you go in, you will find a colt tied up that has never been ridden. Untie it and bring it here. [31] If someone asks you why you are untying it, tell him that the Master needs it."

[32] They went on their way and found everything just as Jesus had told them. [33] As they were untying the colt, its owners said to them, "Why are you untying it?"

[34] "The Master needs it," they answered, [35] and they took the colt to Jesus. Then they threw their cloaks over the animal and helped Jesus get on. [36] As he rode on, people spread their cloaks on the road.

[37] When he came near Jerusalem, at the place where the road went down the Mount of Olives, the large crowd of his disciples began to thank God and praise him in loud voices for all the great things that they had seen: [38] "God bless the king who comes in the name of the Lord! Peace in heaven and glory to God!"

[39] Then some of the Pharisees in the crowd spoke to Jesus. "Teacher," they said, "command your disciples to be quiet!"

[40] Jesus answered, "I tell you that if they keep quiet, the stones themselves will start shouting."

You may also wish to read the full Gospel reading for today: Luke 22:14 – 23:56

Other Readings: Isaiah 50:4-7; Psalm 24; Psalm 47; Philippians 2:6-11

 LECTIO:

We begin Holy Week with Jesus' triumphant entry into Jerusalem. What an occasion it must have been, loaded with symbolic images and meaning.

Jesus' starting point, the Mount of Olives, is significant as it is associated in scripture with the coming of the Lord (Zechariah 14:4).

Luke begins by describing the remarkable provision of a colt for Jesus to ride on. The disciples find everything 'just as Jesus had told them' (verse 32). Luke simply gives us these details without any further comment although Matthew (21:5) interprets this as the fulfilment of Zechariah's prophecy (Zechariah 9:9-10). Zechariah proclaims a King who comes as Saviour on a colt, not with horses and chariots. Jesus is in control and is fully aware of what his last few days on earth will bring.

People spread their cloaks on the road before Jesus, a customary greeting for a victorious king or important person (2 Kings 9:13). They hail 'the king who comes in the name of the Lord' (verse 38) and echo the words of the angels at Jesus' birth (Luke 2:13-14).

This is the last thing the Pharisees wanted to happen. They didn't accept Jesus or his teaching and wanted to prevent others from following him. Nothing could be worse than this noisy hero's welcome. They may also have feared the intervention of the Roman soldiers so they asked Jesus to tell the people to be quiet.

But Jesus' reply (verse 40) indicates that the people's praise was only right and proper. In fact the occasion demanded it. If the people didn't fulfil this requirement then God would cause the very stones of Jerusalem to shout out in praise.

Jesus' dramatic entrance couldn't have come at a worse time for the Pharisees. Jerusalem was packed with pilgrims who had come to celebrate the Passover (Luke 22:7). Matthew (21:10) tells us, 'When Jesus entered Jerusalem, the whole city was thrown into uproar. "Who is he?" the people asked.'

 # MEDITATIO:

- Mingle with the crowd and imagine what this occasion must have been like. Enrich your understanding by reading the accounts from the other Gospel writers in Matthew 21:1-11, Mark 11:1-11 and John 12:12-19.
- Consider the contrast between the humble colt Jesus is riding on and the hero's welcome. What does this tell us?
- Reflect on some of the miracles and 'great things' Jesus had done in his ministry.
- To their credit the disciples followed Jesus' instructions concerning the colt. What can we learn from this? Are you willing to obey God even when you don't fully understand why he is asking you to do something?

 # ORATIO:

Write your own psalm of thanksgiving to Jesus or simply speak out your praise to God for our wonderful Saviour. Today's Psalms can help you get started.

 # CONTEMPLATIO:

Ponder in awe at Jesus' humility revealed so eloquently in Philippians 2:6-11 and worship him proclaiming, 'Jesus Christ is Lord, to the glory of God the Father.'

A SERVANT ATTITUDE

John 13:1-15

[1] It was now the day before the Passover Festival. Jesus knew that the hour had come for him to leave this world and go to the Father. He had always loved those in the world who were his own, and he loved them to the very end.

[2] Jesus and his disciples were at supper. The Devil had already put into the heart of Judas, the son of Simon Iscariot, the thought of betraying Jesus. [3] Jesus knew that the Father had given him complete power; he knew that he had come from God and was going to God. [4] So he rose from the table, took off his outer garment, and tied a towel round his waist. [5] Then he poured some water into a basin and began to wash the disciples' feet and dry them with the towel round his waist.
[6] He came to Simon Peter, who said to him, "Are you going to wash my feet, Lord?"

[7] Jesus answered him, "You do not understand now what I am doing, but you will understand later."

[8] Peter declared, "Never at any time will you wash my feet!"

"If I do not wash your feet," Jesus answered, "you will no longer be my disciple."

[9] Simon Peter answered, "Lord, do not wash only my feet, then! Wash my hands and head, too!"

[10] Jesus said, "Those who have had a bath are completely clean and do not have to wash themselves, except for their feet. All of you are clean – all except one."
[11] (Jesus already knew who was going to betray him; that is why he said, "All of you, except one, are clean.")

[12] After Jesus had washed their feet, he put his outer garment back on and returned to his place at the table. "Do you understand what I have just done to you?" he asked. [13] "You call me Teacher and Lord, and it is right that you do so, because that is what I am. [14] I, your Lord and Teacher, have just washed your feet. You, then, should wash one another's feet. [15] I have set an example for you, so that you will do just what I have done for you.

Other Readings: Exodus 12:1-8, 11-14; Psalm 116:12-13, 15-18;
1 Corinthians 11:23-26

 LECTIO:

John is the only Gospel writer to give us this precious example of Jesus washing the disciples' feet.

By washing their feet Jesus humbles himself in a way that would have shocked the disciples. The host would normally provide water for guests to wash their own feet when entering the house (Luke 7:44). A servant or slave might be given the task, or disciples might possibly wash their teacher's feet, but not the other way round. This was completely unexpected.

This self-humiliation is a deep symbol for the crucifixion of Christ. We cannot gain salvation by our actions. It is by the humble sacrifice of the Son of God that we are saved.

Peter does not understand this sign at first and protests. Jesus insists that Peter must allow him to wash his feet. Peter misunderstands again and wants to be purified completely. What Jesus is looking for here is humility – which is the only way we can receive his gift of salvation.

In this practical action Jesus also demonstrates a very important lesson to the disciples and to us – we must serve one another just as he serves us.

 MEDITATIO:

- Think about what an incredible act of humility this is. The Son of God is washing the feet of his disciples!
- Jesus humbled himself to death on a cross for us. We can do nothing to redeem ourselves. We simply have to respond to God's great love and accept his gift of salvation. Marvel at this wonderful gift.
- Consider how willing you are to serve other Christians in your church. Ask God to help you follow Jesus' example and to show you ways you can serve your fellow Christians.

 ORATIO:

Thank God for the great humility of Jesus who saved us from sin and eternal death. Ask the Holy Spirit to help you overcome pride and selfishness.

Pray the words of Psalm 116:12 as your own prayer today. Listen to anything the Holy Spirit may say to you.

'What can I offer the Lord for all his goodness to me?'

 CONTEMPLATIO:

Spend some time reflecting on Christ's love and humble sacrifice, his painful death for our sake, his never ending desire to be in fellowship with us and to draw us to God the father.

THE OBEDIENT SERVANT

John 18:1-19:42

John 18

¹ After Jesus had said this prayer, he left with his disciples and went across the brook called Kidron. There was a garden in that place, and Jesus and his disciples went in. ² Judas, the traitor, knew where it was, because many times Jesus had met there with his disciples. ³ So Judas went to the garden, taking with him a group of Roman soldiers, and some temple guards sent by the chief priests and the Pharisees; they were armed and carried lanterns and torches. ⁴ Jesus knew everything that was going to happen to him, so he stepped forward and asked them, "Who is it you are looking for?"

⁵ "Jesus of Nazareth," they answered.

"I am he," he said.

Judas, the traitor, was standing there with them. ⁶ When Jesus said to them, "I am he," they moved back and fell to the ground. ⁷ Again Jesus asked them, "Who is it you are looking for?"

"Jesus of Nazareth," they said.

⁸ "I have already told you that I am he," Jesus said. "If, then, you are looking for me, let these others go." ⁹ (He said this so that what he had said might come true: "Father, I have not lost even one of those you gave me.")

¹⁰ Simon Peter, who had a sword, drew it and struck the High Priest's slave, cutting off his right ear. The name of the slave was Malchus. ¹¹ Jesus said to Peter, "Put your sword back in its place! Do you think that I will not drink the cup of suffering which my Father has given me?"

¹² Then the Roman soldiers with their commanding officer and the Jewish guards arrested Jesus, bound him, ¹³ and took him first to Annas. He was the father-in-law of Caiaphas, who was High Priest that year. ¹⁴ It was Caiaphas who had advised the Jewish authorities that it was better that one man should die for all the people.

¹⁵ Simon Peter and another disciple followed Jesus. That other disciple was well known to the High Priest, so he went with Jesus into the courtyard of the High Priest's house, ¹⁶ while Peter stayed outside by the gate. Then the other disciple went back out, spoke to the girl at the gate, and brought Peter inside. ¹⁷ The girl at the gate said to Peter, "Aren't you also one of the disciples of that man?"

"No, I am not," answered Peter.

¹⁸ It was cold, so the servants and guards had built a charcoal fire and were standing round it, warming themselves. So Peter went over and stood with them, warming himself.

¹⁹ The High Priest questioned Jesus about his disciples and about his teaching.

²⁰ Jesus answered, "I have always spoken publicly to everyone; all my teaching was done in the synagogues and in the Temple, where all the people come together.

I have never said anything in secret. ²¹ Why, then, do you question me? Question the people who heard me. Ask them what I told them – they know what I said."

²² When Jesus said this, one of the guards there slapped him and said, "How dare you talk like that to the High Priest!"

²³ Jesus answered him, "If I have said anything wrong, tell everyone here what it was. But if I am right in what I have said, why do you hit me?"

²⁴ Then Annas sent him, still bound, to Caiaphas the High Priest.

²⁵ Peter was still standing there keeping himself warm. So the others said to him, "Aren't you also one of the disciples of that man?"

But Peter denied it. "No, I am not," he said.

²⁶ One of the High Priest's slaves, a relative of the man whose ear Peter had cut off, spoke up. "Didn't I see you with him in the garden?" he asked.

²⁷ Again Peter said "No" – and at once a cock crowed.

²⁸ Early in the morning Jesus was taken from Caiaphas' house to the governor's palace. The Jewish authorities did not go inside the palace, for they wanted to keep themselves ritually clean, in order to be able to eat the Passover meal. ²⁹ So Pilate went outside to them and asked, "What do you accuse this man of?"

³⁰ Their answer was, "We would not have brought him to you if he had not committed a crime."

³¹ Pilate said to them, "Then you yourselves take him and try him according to your own law."

They replied, "We are not allowed to put anyone to death." ³² (This happened in order to make the words of Jesus come true, the words he used when he indicated the kind of death he would die.)

³³ Pilate went back into the palace and called Jesus. "Are you the King of the Jews?" he asked him.

³⁴ Jesus answered, "Does this question come from you or have others told you about me?"

³⁵ Pilate replied, "Do you think I am a Jew? It was your own people and the chief priests who handed you over to me. What have you done?"

³⁶ Jesus said, "My kingdom does not belong to this world; if my kingdom belonged to this world, my followers would fight to keep me from being handed over to the Jewish authorities. No, my kingdom does not belong here!"

³⁷ So Pilate asked him, "Are you a king, then?"

Jesus answered, "You say that I am a king. I was born and came into the world for this one purpose, to speak about the truth. Whoever belongs to the truth listens to me."

³⁸ "And what is truth?" Pilate asked.

Then Pilate went back outside to the people and said to them, "I cannot find any reason to condemn him. ³⁹ But according to the custom you have, I always set free a prisoner for you during the Passover. Do you want me to set free for you the King of the Jews?"

[40] They answered him with a shout, "No, not him! We want Barabbas!" (Barabbas was a bandit.)

John 19

[1] Then Pilate took Jesus and had him whipped. [2] The soldiers made a crown out of thorny branches and put it on his head; then they put a purple robe on him [3] and came to him and said, "Long live the King of the Jews!" And they went up and slapped him.

[4] Pilate went out once more and said to the crowd, "Look, I will bring him out here to you to let you see that I cannot find any reason to condemn him." [5] So Jesus came out, wearing the crown of thorns and the purple robe. Pilate said to them, "Look! Here is the man!"

[6] When the chief priests and the temple guards saw him, they shouted, "Crucify him! Crucify him!"

Pilate said to them, "You take him, then, and crucify him. I find no reason to condemn him."

[7] The crowd answered back, "We have a law that says he ought to die, because he claimed to be the Son of God."

[8] When Pilate heard this, he was even more afraid. [9] He went back into the palace and asked Jesus, "Where do you come from?"

But Jesus did not answer. [10] Pilate said to him, "You will not speak to me? Remember, I have the authority to set you free and also to have you crucified."

[11] Jesus answered, "You have authority over me only because it was given to you by God. So the man who handed me over to you is guilty of a worse sin."

[12] When Pilate heard this, he tried to find a way to set Jesus free. But the crowd shouted back, "If you set him free, that means that you are not the Emperor's friend! Anyone who claims to be a king is a rebel against the Emperor!"

[13] When Pilate heard these words, he took Jesus outside and sat down on the judge's seat in the place called "The Stone Pavement". (In Hebrew the name is "Gabbatha".) [14] It was then almost noon of the day before the Passover. Pilate said to the people, "Here is your king!"

[15] They shouted back, "Kill him! Kill him! Crucify him!"

Pilate asked them, "Do you want me to crucify your king?"

The chief priests answered, "The only king we have is the Emperor!"

[16] Then Pilate handed Jesus over to them to be crucified.

So they took charge of Jesus. [17] He went out, carrying his cross, and came to "The Place of the Skull", as it is called. (In Hebrew it is called "Golgotha".) [18] There they crucified him; and they also crucified two other men, one on each side, with Jesus between them. [19] Pilate wrote a notice and had it put on the cross. "Jesus of Nazareth, the King of the Jews", is what he wrote. [20] Many people read it, because the place where Jesus was crucified was not far from the city. The notice was written in Hebrew, Latin, and Greek. [21] The chief priests said to Pilate, "Do not write 'The

King of the Jews', but rather, 'This man said, I am the King of the Jews.' "

^{22} Pilate answered, "What I have written stays written."

^{23} After the soldiers had crucified Jesus, they took his clothes and divided them into four parts, one part for each soldier. They also took the robe, which was made of one piece of woven cloth without any seams in it. ^{24} The soldiers said to one another, "Let's not tear it; let's throw dice to see who will get it." This happened in order to make the scripture come true:

"They divided my clothes among themselves and gambled for my robe."

And this is what the soldiers did.

^{25} Standing close to Jesus' cross were his mother, his mother's sister, Mary the wife of Clopas, and Mary Magdalene. ^{26} Jesus saw his mother and the disciple he loved standing there; so he said to his mother, "He is your son."

^{27} Then he said to the disciple, "She is your mother." From that time the disciple took her to live in his home.

^{28} Jesus knew that by now everything had been completed; and in order to make the scripture come true, he said, "I am thirsty."

^{29} A bowl was there, full of cheap wine; so a sponge was soaked in the wine, put on a stalk of hyssop, and lifted up to his lips. ^{30} Jesus drank the wine and said, "It is finished!"

Then he bowed his head and died.

^{31} Then the Jewish authorities asked Pilate to allow them to break the legs of the men who had been crucified, and to take the bodies down from the crosses. They requested this because it was Friday, and they did not want the bodies to stay on the crosses on the Sabbath, since the coming Sabbath was especially holy. ^{32} So the soldiers went and broke the legs of the first man and then of the other man who had been crucified with Jesus. ^{33} But when they came to Jesus, they saw that he was already dead, so they did not break his legs. ^{34} One of the soldiers, however, plunged his spear into Jesus' side, and at once blood and water poured out. ^{35} (The one who saw this happen has spoken of it, so that you also may believe. What he said is true, and he knows that he speaks the truth.) ^{36} This was done to make the scripture come true: "Not one of his bones will be broken." ^{37} And there is another scripture that says, "People will look at him whom they pierced."

^{38} After this, Joseph, who was from the town of Arimathea, asked Pilate if he could take Jesus' body. (Joseph was a follower of Jesus, but in secret, because he was afraid of the Jewish authorities.) Pilate told him he could have the body, so Joseph went and took it away. ^{39} Nicodemus, who at first had gone to see Jesus at night, went with Joseph, taking with him about 30 kilogrammes of spices, a mixture of myrrh and aloes. ^{40} The two men took Jesus' body and wrapped it in linen with the spices according to the Jewish custom of preparing a body for burial.

^{41} There was a garden in the place where Jesus had been put to death, and in it there was a new tomb where no one had ever been buried. ^{42} Since it was the day before the Sabbath and because the tomb was close by, they placed Jesus' body there.

THE OBEDIENT SERVANT

John 18:1-19:42

Other Readings: Isaiah 52:13-53:12; Psalm 31:1, 5, 11-12, 14-16, 24;
Hebrews 4:14-16, 5:7-9

 LECTIO:

John provides us with a compelling account of Jesus' passion. He gives us a different perspective to the other Gospel writers.

Jesus is shown suffering at the hands of the powers of this world (18:12, 22; 19:1-3). Throughout all the trials Jesus remains in charge of the situation. He is the judge of those who now judge him but he submits voluntarily to their authority at this time (19:17).

John includes an instruction from Jesus to 'the disciple he loved' - a reference to John himself (John 21:24) - to look after his mother. This shows Jesus' concern for his mother's welfare even from the cross.

John also writes about the soldier piercing Jesus' side with a spear instead of breaking his legs as in the case of the two others that were crucified with him (19:32-34). John explains 'this was done to make the scripture come true' referring to Psalm 34:20 and Zechariah 12:10.

We are also told that when Jesus' side was pierced 'blood and water poured out'. On a literal level this is conclusive proof that Jesus was dead, answering sceptics who later tried to deny the resurrection on the basis that Jesus was not actually dead. Some also suggest that on a symbolic level the blood and water represent Baptism and the Holy Eucharist.

Then we meet Joseph of Arimathea, who asks Pilate for Jesus' body, and Nicodemus (19:38-40). The two men bury Jesus in a new tomb close to where he died. They were both important Jewish council members and also secret disciples of Jesus. Jesus had spoken to Nicodemus about his death and his words include one of the Bible's most famous verses, John 3:16:

'For God loved the world so much that he gave his only Son, so that everyone who believes in him may not die but have eternal life.'

MEDITATIO:

- What do we learn about Jesus from this Passion narrative? What touches you most?
- Consider why Jesus endured the pain and humiliation of death on the cross.
- What did Jesus mean when he said 'it is finished'? What is the significance of this for you today?
- Two other characters, Peter and Pilate, feature strongly in these two chapters. What do we learn about them?

 ORATIO:

'Let us be brave, then, and approach God's throne, where there is grace. There we will receive mercy and find grace to help us just when we need it.' Hebrews 4:16

Before you pray today read the verses the liturgy offers us from Hebrews. They explain why we can dare to come before Almighty God in prayer and tell us that Jesus is 'the source of eternal salvation'. Consider these words and make your own response to God.

 CONTEMPLATIO:

Isaiah 53 spells out what Jesus did for us. Take some time to read through this moving portrait of the 'suffering servant'. Verses 5, 6 and 7 remind us Jesus was pierced for our faults, crushed for our sins. His suffering brings us peace and we are healed, though we were like sheep gone astray. Jesus bore it all humbly, never opening his mouth. Spend some time marvelling at all Jesus accomplished for us at Calvary.

HE IS RISEN

John 20:1-9

[1] Early on Sunday morning, while it was still dark, Mary Magdalene went to the tomb and saw that the stone had been taken away from the entrance. [2] She went running to Simon Peter and the other disciple, whom Jesus loved, and told them, "They have taken the Lord from the tomb, and we don't know where they have put him!"

[3] Then Peter and the other disciple went to the tomb. [4] The two of them were running, but the other disciple ran faster than Peter and reached the tomb first. [5] He bent over and saw the linen wrappings, but he did not go in. [6] Behind him came Simon Peter, and he went straight into the tomb. He saw the linen wrappings lying there [7] and the cloth which had been round Jesus' head. It was not lying with the linen wrappings but was rolled up by itself. [8] Then the other disciple, who had reached the tomb first, also went in; he saw and believed. [9] (They still did not understand the scripture which said that he must rise from death.)

Other Readings: Acts 10:34, 37-43; Psalm 118:1-2, 16-17, 22-23; Colossians 3:1-4

 LECTIO:

This is a compelling narrative. Jesus' body has disappeared and Mary Magdalene is first on the scene. You can read about her encounter with Jesus in the verses following today's reading.

This passage focuses mainly on the two disciples, Peter and another whom tradition identifies as the apostle John.

The narrator tells us that John believes Jesus is risen as soon as he sees the abandoned linen in the grave. What causes John to believe Jesus is alive? Some commentators believe it was the folding of the grave clothes in a particular style – Jesus' style, one that John recognised. Whoever had done this was not dead but alive. Surely this must be Jesus. This is John's first encounter with the risen Christ.

Did John share his belief with Peter? We don't know. All we are told is that the disciples still did not understand the scripture which said Jesus must rise from the dead. This would soon change. But for each person it was a slightly different experience.

Mary Magdalene, Peter, John and the other disciples meet Jesus face to face in the verses following today's reading in John's account.

The eye witness accounts of these disciples are fundamental to the faith of Christians. They knew that Jesus died on the cross, they knew precisely where he was buried and each personally met with the risen Christ. These encounters with the risen Lord confirmed their belief that he was indeed who he said he was - the promised Messiah, the Son of God.

 # MEDITATIO:

- Picture yourself on that first morning after Jesus' crucifixion. Waking up, trying to eat and drink, and going with Mary Magdalene or Peter and John to the tomb. What would you think and feel? And by contrast, how would you feel going to bed that night?
- Think about how you might explain to a friend who doesn't follow Jesus why the events that took place that first Easter are still so important today.

 # ORATIO:

Today is one of the most joyful in the church calendar. The words of the other gospel writers 'He is not here; he has been raised' (Matthew 28:6) echo down the centuries. Bring your own praise and express your joy and thanks to God. Use the verses from Psalm 118 to help you.

 # CONTEMPLATIO:

'You have been raised to life with Christ, so set your hearts on the things that are in heaven, where Christ sits on his throne at the right-hand side of God.'

Colossians 3:1-4 tells us that in Christ we have experienced our own 'resurrection' into a new spiritual life. Spend some time reflecting on what it means to have your life 'hidden with Christ in God' and setting your heart and mind on heaven instead of earthly concerns.

MY LORD AND MY GOD

John 20:19-31

¹⁹ It was late that Sunday evening, and the disciples were gathered together behind locked doors, because they were afraid of the Jewish authorities. Then Jesus came and stood among them. "Peace be with you," he said. ²⁰ After saying this, he showed them his hands and his side. The disciples were filled with joy at seeing the Lord. ²¹ Jesus said to them again, "Peace be with you. As the Father sent me, so I send you." ²² Then he breathed on them and said, "Receive the Holy Spirit. ²³ If you forgive people's sins, they are forgiven; if you do not forgive them, they are not forgiven."

²⁴ One of the twelve disciples, Thomas (called the Twin), was not with them when Jesus came. ²⁵ So the other disciples told him, "We have seen the Lord!"

Thomas said to them, "Unless I see the scars of the nails in his hands and put my finger on those scars and my hand in his side, I will not believe."

²⁶ A week later the disciples were together again indoors, and Thomas was with them. The doors were locked, but Jesus came and stood among them and said, "Peace be with you." ²⁷ Then he said to Thomas, "Put your finger here, and look at my hands; then stretch out your hand and put it in my side. Stop your doubting, and believe!"

²⁸ Thomas answered him, "My Lord and my God!"

²⁹ Jesus said to him, "Do you believe because you see me? How happy are those who believe without seeing me!"

³⁰ In his disciples' presence Jesus performed many other miracles which are not written down in this book. ³¹ But these have been written in order that you may believe that Jesus is the Messiah, the Son of God, and that through your faith in him you may have life.

Other Readings: Acts 5:12-16; Psalm 118:2-4, 22-27; Revelation 1:9-13, 17-19

 LECTIO:

Once again John takes us behind closed doors to share a precious encounter with the risen Christ. Many similar accounts circulated among the Christians living in Jerusalem after his death in about 30 AD. The gospel writers used these same stories for teaching.

Today we are bystanders at a Sunday meeting of the disciples. Suddenly Jesus appears and the disciples are overjoyed. Jesus sends them to spread the gospel, gives them authority to forgive sins and breathes on them to receive the Holy Spirit.

Unfortunately, one of the twelve disciples, Thomas, was not there to share the experience. When the others tell him they have seen the living Lord Jesus, he doesn't believe them. Rather brashly he declares he will only believe if he can touch the nail scars in Jesus' hands and the wound in his side.

The community meet again the next Sunday. This time Thomas is with them. The Lord appears and greets them. Shockingly, he invites Thomas to probe his wounds by putting his fingers in the torn hands and his entire hand in the hole in Jesus' side.

Confronted with the undeniable reality of Jesus' presence Thomas is overwhelmed and declares Jesus to be his Lord and his God.

Thomas made a confession of faith because he saw the risen Christ. And Jesus looks ahead to all those who will come after and believe without seeing him physically.

 MEDITATIO:

- Imagine the joy and excitement that the disciples must have felt when they saw the risen Jesus.
- Thomas' faith was ignited as he saw the risen Lord. Do you believe or are you looking for further proof before you can accept Jesus as your living Lord?
- Jesus said to his disciples 'Peace be with you'. Consider the significance of these reassuring words.

 ORATIO:

'My Lord and my God'. This was Thomas's declaration of faith. It is a simple yet profound prayer. Can you make it your own and pray it throughout this coming week? Be open to God speaking to you as you make your own confession of faith and trust in him.

 CONTEMPLATIO:

We continue to celebrate the resurrection of Jesus. Consider the verses from Psalm 118:

'His love is eternal.' (verse 4)

'The stone which the builders rejected as worthless turned out to be the most important of all. This was done by the Lord; what a wonderful sight it is! This is the day of the Lord's victory; let us be happy, let us celebrate.' (verses 22-24)

DO YOU LOVE ME?

John 21:1-19

[1] After this, Jesus appeared once more to his disciples at Lake Tiberias. This is how it happened. [2] Simon Peter, Thomas (called the Twin), Nathanael (the one from Cana in Galilee), the sons of Zebedee, and two other disciples of Jesus were all together. [3] Simon Peter said to the others, "I am going fishing."

"We will come with you," they told him. So they went out in a boat, but all that night they did not catch a thing. [4] As the sun was rising, Jesus stood at the water's edge, but the disciples did not know that it was Jesus. [5] Then he asked them, "Young men, haven't you caught anything?"

"Not a thing," they answered.

[6] He said to them, "Throw your net out on the right side of the boat, and you will catch some." So they threw the net out and could not pull it back in, because they had caught so many fish.

[7] The disciple whom Jesus loved said to Peter, "It is the Lord!" When Peter heard that it was the Lord, he wrapped his outer garment round him (for he had taken his clothes off) and jumped into the water. [8] The other disciples came to shore in the boat, pulling the net full of fish. They were not very far from land, about a hundred metres away. [9] When they stepped ashore, they saw a charcoal fire there with fish on it and some bread. [10] Then Jesus said to them, "Bring some of the fish you have just caught."

[11] Simon Peter went aboard and dragged the net ashore full of big fish, 153 in all; even though there were so many, still the net did not tear. [12] Jesus said to them, "Come and eat." None of the disciples dared ask him, "Who are you?" because they knew it was the Lord. [13] So Jesus went over, took the bread, and gave it to them; he did the same with the fish.

[14] This, then, was the third time Jesus appeared to the disciples after he was raised from death.

[15] After they had eaten, Jesus said to Simon Peter, "Simon son of John, do you love me more than these others do?"

"Yes, Lord," he answered, "you know that I love you."

Jesus said to him, "Take care of my lambs." [16] A second time Jesus said to him, "Simon son of John, do you love me?"

"Yes, Lord," he answered, "you know that I love you."

Jesus said to him, "Take care of my sheep." [17] A third time Jesus said, "Simon son of John, do you love me?"

Peter was sad because Jesus asked him the third time, "Do you love me?" so he said to him, "Lord, you know everything; you know that I love you!"

Jesus said to him, "Take care of my sheep. [18] I am telling you the truth: when you were young, you used to get ready and go anywhere you wanted to; but when you are old, you will stretch out your hands and someone else will bind you and take you where you don't want to go." ¹⁹ (In saying this, Jesus was indicating the way in which Peter would die and bring glory to God.) Then Jesus said to him, "Follow me!"

Other Readings: Acts 5:27-32, 40-41; Psalm 30:1, 3-5, 10-12; Revelation 5:11-14

 # LECTIO:

Realising Jesus is on the beach Peter literally plunges in, this time leaping overboard in his eagerness to get to the Lord.

Jesus has some important words for Peter. He wanted first to hear Peter's confession of love. Jesus really tested him by asking him three times, 'do you love me?' It's a painful reminder of Peter's denials of Jesus. Then Jesus commits his mission to Peter, 'take care of my sheep'.

 # MEDITATIO:

- Consider Jesus' great mercy towards Peter. Although Peter denied him, Jesus gave him the opportunity to be restored and fulfil his calling to lead the early church.
- Compare Peter's response here to his response in Luke 5:4-8 when there was another remarkable catch of fish. What has changed?

 # ORATIO:

Imagine Jesus is asking you the question, 'do you love me?' Spend some time with the Lord and make your own response.

 # CONTEMPLATIO:

'To him who sits on the throne and to the Lamb, be praise and honour, glory and might, for ever and ever!'

John gives us a glimpse of heaven in Revelation 5:11-14. Read through these verses several times and bring your own worship and adoration before the throne.

FOLLOWING THE SHEPHERD

John 10:27-30

[27] My sheep listen to my voice; I know them, and they follow me. [28] I give them eternal life, and they shall never die. No one can snatch them away from me. [29] What my Father has given me is greater than everything, and no one can snatch them away from the Father's care. [30] The Father and I are one."

Other Readings: Acts 13:14, 43-52; Psalm 100:1-3, 5; Revelation 7:9, 14-17

 LECTIO:

These few verses form part of a longer passage in which John reports a lively debate between Jesus and the people about his relationship to God the Father.

It ended with the people wanting to stone Jesus! When Jesus challenged their murderous intentions they answered, 'We do not want to stone you because of any good deeds, but because of your blasphemy! You are only a man, but you are trying to make yourself God!'(John 10:33).

Jesus sees deeper into their hearts than they realised. He knew they would not accept him 'for they are not my sheep' (verse 26). And they were not his sheep because the Father had not given them to him as his believers.

Jesus hints at the mysterious gift and wonderful grace of faith. No one can believe in Jesus unless he is given the grace by the Father.

In John 6 Jesus conveys this idea in another way. Jesus told his puzzled listeners that he was the bread of God and they needed to feed on him if they wanted to live (John 6:25-59). Once again the gracious gift of God is needed for faith to believe. And the Father is the sole giver of grace.

If God the Father gifts an individual with grace, that person belongs to Jesus and becomes one of Jesus' 'sheep'. They are given the ability to grow in understanding of all that Jesus teaches and to receive eternal life. But for growth to occur we need to be in constant touch with Jesus.

The people who wanted to stone Jesus had not yet received the Father's gift of faith. If their hearts and minds were open, they would have seen that this was an opportunity to seek the Father's help and grace to believe. But the 'goats' declined (Matthew 25:32) and refused to accept Jesus as God's Son.

In this age of uncertainties we can have no stronger promise than the one Jesus gives to those who follow him: no one and nothing can separate us from God. This is explained further in Romans 8:38-39. It is the truth – nothing can separate us from the love of God that is ours in Christ Jesus. This promise is not only for this life but extends beyond our death into eternity.

 # MEDITATIO:

- In these few verses Jesus mentions several benefits of being one of his sheep. Think about what each one means to you.
- As Christians we believe that God knows everything, but sometimes we act and pray as though he doesn't. In verse 27 Jesus reminds us that he knows each of his sheep individually. Do you find this reassuring or uncomfortable? Consider your response to this.
- 'My sheep listen to my voice… and they follow me.' How good are you at listening to Jesus' voice and doing what he says? Ask Jesus what would be best for you to do to help you be more obedient.
- If faith in Jesus is a gift from the Father, how should this influence our attitude to people who don't believe in Jesus?

 # ORATIO:

Bring what God reveals to you from this passage and your time of meditation to him in prayer. Don't rush this – take your time.

Read Psalm 100 and use this to give thanks to God for giving you the gift of faith in Jesus.

 # CONTEMPLATIO:

Have you considered that as a believer you are the gift of the Father to his Son, Jesus? Think about your relationship with Jesus your shepherd.

LOVE ONE ANOTHER

John 13:31-35

[31] After Judas had left, Jesus said, "Now the Son of Man's glory is revealed; now God's glory is revealed through him. [32] And if God's glory is revealed through him, then God will reveal the glory of the Son of Man in himself, and he will do so at once. [33] My children, I shall not be with you very much longer. You will look for me; but I tell you now what I told the Jewish authorities, 'You cannot go where I am going.' [34] And now I give you a new commandment: love one another. As I have loved you, so you must love one another. [35] If you have love for one another, then everyone will know that you are my disciples."

Other Readings: Acts 14:21-27; Psalm 145:8-13; Revelation 21:1-5

 LECTIO:

Today we are with Jesus and his disciples in the upper room at the Last Supper. John does not describe the 'Eucharistic meal' itself like the other gospel writers but provides different insights into Jesus' life and teaching.

Jesus waits until after Judas has left before revealing a 'new' commandment to his disciples. Knowing what Judas was harbouring in his heart it is not surprising that Jesus chooses to speak about this after he has left.

What is so special about this 'new' commandment? The requirement to love God and to love our neighbour as ourself would already have been well known to the disciples from the Law of Moses (Deuteronomy 6:5 and Leviticus 19:18). But Jesus' teaching and example of love deepen these commands. In the other three Gospels this teaching is often referred to as 'The Great Commandment' (Matthew 22:34-40, Mark 12:28-34, Luke 10:25-28).

The new challenge Jesus lays before his disciples here is to love each other 'as I have loved you'. Jesus proclaims that God now makes known the divine identity and authority of the Son of Man, who is Jesus himself. Jesus' love for his disciples, for us, and for all people reflects the unconditional mutual love that exists between God the Father, Son and Holy Spirit.

Christians, living out this mutual love in their everyday lives make God's mystical love a concrete fact to people around them and demonstrate they are Jesus' followers. In practising this unconditional love ordinary Christians draw back a veil to reveal a glimpse of heaven and the love flooding from the Holy Trinity.

Now we can see why Jesus and John place such a great emphasis upon the relationship between the persons of the Holy Trinity (John 14-16). And this is why Jesus insists that the love shared between Christians has to be modelled upon his own love towards them: self-sacrificing and unconditional.

MEDITATIO:

- What strikes you most from these verses? Ask the Holy Spirit to speak to you.
- How do you feel about Jesus' command to love other Christians as Jesus loves us?
- Does Jesus ask the impossible? How can we try to obey this command? Who can we go to for help?
- Consider whether there are any ways God might want you to express his love to another Christian.

ORATIO:

Psalm 145:8-13 lists some of the characteristics of God. As God chips away at our worldliness to reveal his image and likeness we will start to reflect his nature. Prayerfully offer these verses to God.

Open your heart to God and let him speak to you. If you are experiencing difficulties in a particular relationship then bring this before the Lord.

CONTEMPLATIO:

Revelation 21:1-5 speaks of the 'new heaven and earth'. Consider this promise and think about the links between Jesus' new commandment and this vision. Think about how Jesus is clothing us, as the Church, to be his bride.

TRUSTING JESUS

John 14:23-29

²³ Jesus answered him, "Whoever loves me will obey my teaching. My Father will love him, and my Father and I will come to him and live with him. ²⁴ Whoever does not love me does not obey my teaching. And the teaching you have heard is not mine, but comes from the Father, who sent me.

²⁵ "I have told you this while I am still with you. ²⁶ The Helper, the Holy Spirit, whom the Father will send in my name, will teach you everything and make you remember all that I have told you.

²⁷ "Peace is what I leave with you; it is my own peace that I give you. I do not give it as the world does. Do not be worried and upset; do not be afraid. ²⁸ You heard me say to you, 'I am leaving, but I will come back to you.' If you loved me, you would be glad that I am going to the Father; for he is greater than I. ²⁹ I have told you this now before it all happens, so that when it does happen, you will believe.

Other Readings: Acts 15:1-2, 22-29; Psalm 67:1-2, 4-5, 7; Revelation 21:10-14, 22-23

 LECTIO:

This week we continue to read about the teaching Jesus gave to his disciples in the context of the Last Supper (John 14-17). Today's text is a response to a question from another disciple called Judas. (John 13:31-35 makes it clear this is not Judas Iscariot as he had left them earlier to betray Jesus.)

Jesus has just said that he will reveal himself to those who love him (verse 21). Judas is puzzled. Is Jesus saying he will only reveal himself to the disciples? Jesus doesn't answer Judas directly even though it is apparent his understanding is very limited. Jesus knows the disciples will get more insight after his resurrection. So for now he emphasises again his relationship to God the Father. He stresses that his teaching comes direct from the Father and that the critical point is for each one to put his teaching into action.

But Jesus makes it plain he doesn't expect us to be able to do this on our own. God the Father is going to send us a helper. The Holy Spirit is going to teach us everything we need to know to live, love and serve Jesus.

Jesus tells them he will be leaving them to go to the Father. He doesn't reveal just how soon this will be or explain the shocking nature of his death. But he does seek to reassure them. He promises them he will come back for them, that they won't be left on their own but will have the Holy Spirit to help them and he leaves his peace with them.

Jesus wants them to trust him. Even though they don't understand everything now, later they will see what he was saying and believe in him.

MEDITATIO:

- Why does Jesus put so much emphasis on living out the gospel message to express your love for him?
- How easy do you find it to trust God when you don't get the answers you expect or you don't understand things? What can we learn from this passage to help us?
- How do you relate to the Holy Spirit? Do you ask for his help to put Jesus' teaching into practice in your life?
- How does Jesus leave us his peace?

ORATIO:

Thank God for sending Jesus and the Holy Spirit. Ask God to speak to you and show you how he wants you to respond to him today. This may be out of a word or phrase from the Scripture passage or it maybe something prompted by one of the questions above. Take your time.

CONTEMPLATIO:

Think about how much God loves you and how he has shown his love for you. Marvel at the wonderful promise that the Father and Jesus come to live with us.

UNITY WITH GOD

John 17:20-26

[20] "I pray not only for them, but also for those who believe in me because of their message. [21] I pray that they may all be one. Father! May they be in us, just as you are in me and I am in you. May they be one, so that the world will believe that you sent me. [22] I gave them the same glory you gave me, so that they may be one, just as you and I are one: [23] I in them and you in me, so that they may be completely one, in order that the world may know that you sent me and that you love them as you love me.

[24] "Father! You have given them to me, and I want them to be with me where I am, so that they may see my glory, the glory you gave me; for you loved me before the world was made. [25] Righteous Father! The world does not know you, but I know you, and these know that you sent me. [26] I made you known to them, and I will continue to do so, in order that the love you have for me may be in them, and so that I also may be in them."

Other Readings: Acts 7:55-60; Psalm 97:1-2, 6-7, 9; Revelation 22:12-14, 16-17, 20

 LECTIO:

Today we share part of what has come to be known as Jesus' 'High Priestly Prayer'. This is the jewel and the final part of Jesus' teaching for his disciples before his passion.

Unity is at the heart of this prayer. Jesus prays repeatedly that his disciples will experience the same unity that he enjoys with the Father. And this prayer is not just for those disciples that were with him that evening. This unity isn't limited in any way by time or space. It is for all his believers for all time.

It is a mystery of God's grace that frail human beings can be in such unity. Two things however seem to be essential. Firstly, to be in relationship and unity with God the Father and with Jesus: 'may they be in us' (verse 21). Secondly, to have God's unconditional love in us: 'that the love you have for me may be in them' (verse 26).

This unity has a glorious purpose - to draw others to God the Father through Jesus. Through this unity people will believe that God loves them and sent Jesus to save them.

Jesus' prayer is bold and daring, but then he knows, as did the angel Gabriel who brought the news of his birth to Mary, that 'there is nothing that God cannot do.' (Luke 1:37).

 # MEDITATIO:

- What does this passage reveal about the relationship between God the Father, Jesus and his disciples?
- Why do you think unity is so important to Jesus? What has been your experience of unity in your church and with other Christians? What things hinder unity with others in your church community?
- When are you most aware of the presence of Jesus within your church?
- Does your relationship with God give you the freedom to make bold prayer requests like Jesus? If not, consider why this might be.

 # ORATIO:

Sit down and spend a while in silence. Let God speak to you and lead you to respond to him in prayer. He may encourage you to be daring and ask something that you've not had the courage to ask before because humanly speaking it seems impossible. He may direct you to pray about a relationship that needs reconciliation or for someone to believe in Jesus and know that God loves them.

 # CONTEMPLATIO:

Consider the words 'the love you have for me (Jesus) may be in them' from Jesus' prayer (verse 26). Think about how much God the Father loves Jesus.

Now consider what it means to have God's unconditional love in you. How does this affect your relationship with God? Does it overflow into your relationships with others?

DIVINE HELP

John 14:15-16, 23-26

[15] "If you love me, you will obey my commandments. [16] I will ask the Father, and he will give you another Helper, who will stay with you for ever.

[23] Jesus answered him, "Whoever loves me will obey my teaching. My Father will love him, and my Father and I will come to him and live with him. [24] Whoever does not love me does not obey my teaching. And the teaching you have heard is not mine, but comes from the Father, who sent me.

[25] "I have told you this while I am still with you. [26] The Helper, the Holy Spirit, whom the Father will send in my name, will teach you everything and make you remember all that I have told you.

Other Readings: Acts 2:1-11; Psalm 104:1, 24, 29-31, 34; Romans 8:8-17

 LECTIO:

We return to the gospel passage we read two weeks ago along with verses 15-16 from earlier in the chapter. This teaching is so important that Jesus repeats it to help his first disciples remember it and put it into practice. Today we too have another opportunity to consider the significance of Jesus' words.

Jesus asks the disciples to love him. Easy enough to say 'yes', you might think. But Jesus makes it clear that loving him takes far more than a simple word. Love in Jesus eyes has a very practical outcome and it takes the shape of obedience to his commandments.

Jesus continues with an amazing promise for everyone who obeys him. Both the Father and Jesus will come and live with them. Jesus does not explain exactly what this 'living with' will be like but it surely indicates a very special and intimate personal relationship.

At this point Jesus makes it clear that these words are not his own idea. This teaching comes directly from God the Father, which is of course equally true of all Jesus' words.

Jesus now talks about the helper, who he reveals as the Holy Spirit. Sometimes the Holy Spirit is overlooked as people deepen their relationships with Jesus and the Father. But he plays a huge part in our relationship with Jesus. In this reading he is revealed to be a teacher and helper for the disciples, reminding them of Jesus' teaching and helping them to understand and live it.

Perhaps in another sense the Holy Spirit is Jesus' helper too. He continues the work Jesus started in the lives of the first disciples and in us today, now that Jesus has returned to his Father.

Jesus also repeats to the disciples that he will ask the Father to send the Holy Spirit to help them after he returns to heaven and promises that the Holy Spirit will stay with them forever.

 # MEDITATIO:

- Consider the role of God the Father in this passage.
- Which words of Jesus strike you most from today's readings?
- How do you respond to this connection between love and obedience?
- Do you find some areas of Jesus' teaching difficult to obey and put into practice in your life? What can you do about this?
- Consider the importance of the Holy Spirit in your everyday life. Read Romans 8:1-17. Think about what this means for you.

 # ORATIO:

Today we remember the dramatic way the Holy Spirit filled the first disciples on the day of Pentecost. Prayerfully read Acts 2:1-11 and give thanks to God for sending us the Holy Spirit to be our helper.

Each day this week, ask the Holy Spirit to fill you afresh and help you to live in a way that will please Jesus. It's only with the Holy Spirit's help that we can obediently love and serve Jesus.

 # CONTEMPLATIO:

'For the Spirit that God has given you does not make you slaves and cause you to be afraid; instead, the Spirit makes you God's children, and by the Spirit's power we cry out to God, Father! My Father!' Romans 8:15

Consider what an incredible privilege it is to be able to call Almighty God our Father and what it means to be his children.

REVEALING THE TRUTH

John 16:12-15

¹²"I have much more to tell you, but now it would be too much for you to bear. ¹³ When, however, the Spirit comes, who reveals the truth about God, he will lead you into all the truth. He will not speak on his own authority, but he will speak of what he hears, and will tell you of things to come. ¹⁴ He will give me glory, because he will take what I say and tell it to you. ¹⁵ All that my Father has is mine; that is why I said that the Spirit will take what I give him and tell it to you.

Other Readings: Proverbs 8:22-31; Psalm 8:3-8; Romans 5:1-5

 LECTIO:

We are very much in the heart of Jesus' teachings during the Last Supper. Jesus has so much to say to prepare his faithful band of disciples for the traumatic events that lay immediately ahead of them.

The Holy Spirit continues to be in the spotlight. Here Jesus teaches that the role of the Holy Spirit is to 'reveal the truth about God', to 'lead you into all the truth' and 'tell you of things to come' (verse 13).

Jesus could have explained more to his disciples at this point about what is going to happen but he knows that they would not be able to take any more in. So he chooses instead to give them glimpses of the work of the Holy Spirit. After Jesus' resurrection the Holy Spirit will help the disciples understand what they need to know in order to live in relationship with God and give them the power they need to do so (Acts 1:8).

Jesus explains more about the relationship between the Holy Spirit, the Father and himself. The Holy Spirit helps us understand and see the truth about God and guides us. In this way he brings glory to the Father and the Son. The three members of the Holy Trinity are one in complete unity.

MEDITATIO:

- Think about the phrase 'the truth about God'. What does this mean to you?
- Do we still need the Holy Spirit to work in our lives today? What does this passage teach us about how the Holy Spirit can help us?
- How would you feel if you gave someone a gift which they largely ignored? Can we sometimes be guilty of ignoring or taking for granted this precious gift from God?
- What can we learn about the inner life of the Holy Trinity from today's reading?

 ORATIO:

'... for God has poured out his love into our hearts by means of the Holy Spirit, who is God's gift to us.' Romans 5:5

Thank God for his love for you and for giving you the gift of the Holy Spirit. Ask God to help you appreciate this love more deeply and be willing to share his love with people around you.

Have you experienced a special time in prayer or reading the Scriptures when the Holy Spirit reveals something new to you? Ask God to do that this week.

 CONTEMPLATIO:

Have you ever looked at the vastness of the sky, the sea or a landscape and felt very small in comparison?

Spend some time now marvelling with the Psalmist at why the creator of the whole universe should care for you and me.

'When I look at the sky, which you have made,
    at the moon and the stars, which you set in their places –
what are human beings, that you care for them;
    mere mortals, that you care for them?
Yet you made them inferior only to yourself;
    you crowned them with glory and honour.
You appointed them rulers over everything you made;
    you placed them over all creation:' Psalm 8:3-6

GOD COMES TO SAVE

Luke 7:11-17

[11] Soon afterwards Jesus went to a town called Nain, accompanied by his disciples and a large crowd. [12] Just as he arrived at the gate of the town, a funeral procession was coming out. The dead man was the only son of a woman who was a widow, and a large crowd from the town was with her. [13] When the Lord saw her, his heart was filled with pity for her, and he said to her, "Don't cry." [14] Then he walked over and touched the coffin, and the men carrying it stopped. Jesus said, "Young man! Get up, I tell you!" [15] The dead man sat up and began to talk, and Jesus gave him back to his mother.

[16] They all were filled with fear and praised God. "A great prophet has appeared among us!" they said; "God has come to save his people!"

[17] This news about Jesus went out through all the country and the surrounding territory.

Other Readings: 1 Kings 17:17-24; Psalm 30:1, 3-5, 10-12; Galatians 1:11-19

 LECTIO:

Can you imagine this scene in a small town near Nazareth? A large crowd, women wailing and a funeral procession is passing by. The chief mourner is an older woman.

This poor woman has already lost her husband. Now her only child is dead and all her future security has died with him. She is left behind with no one to provide for even her most basic needs. Her grief is pain-filled and raw.

Jesus joins the sympathetic crowd. No one asks him to intervene but compassion moves him to act. He touches the makeshift coffin, probably no more than a plank used to carry the dead body for burial.

This tiny action made Jesus ceremonially unclean and would have shocked those around him. The procession comes to a halt. Jesus tells the dead body to get up. The young man sits up and starts to talk! Jesus 'gives him back to his mother'. Luke repeats this exact phrase from 1 Kings 17:23 describing the miraculous raising of another widow's son – this time by Elijah.

The people don't know who to look at first - the man raised back to life, his ecstatic mother or Jesus, who right in front of their very eyes has repeated the miracle performed by one of their greatest prophets, Elijah.

Fear and praise grip the crowd at the same time. They echo the words of Zechariah's prophecy about the Messiah (Luke 1:67-75), 'God has come to save his people!'

This event takes on added significance when seen in context. Read the verses before and after it in Luke 7. This miracle follows straight after the healing of the Roman officer's servant, when Jesus was amazed at the officer's great faith. Jesus demonstrated his authority over sickness and the servant was healed.

In the verses after today's Gospel reading two of John the Baptist's disciples arrive. They have been sent by John to establish if Jesus is the long-awaited Messiah. Jesus simply tells them to report what is happening – people are being healed, the dead raised and the gospel is being preached. Jesus knew John would make the connection with the Messianic prophecies he was fulfilling such as Isaiah 35:5.

 MEDITATIO:

- Imagine you were one of the mourners that witnessed this once in a lifetime miracle. What would you have thought about Jesus after seeing this miracle?
- The verses that precede today's reading highlight Jesus' authority over sickness. This miracle demonstrates that Jesus has authority over death. Why is this significant?

 ORATIO:

The widow didn't ask Jesus to help her but he chose to intervene. Think about the times Jesus has intervened in your life to help you. Take some time to express your thanks and praise to God.

The Psalmist gives his testimony in Psalm 30. Let these words inspire your prayers too.

 CONTEMPLATIO:

In Galatians 1:11-19 we read how God revealed Jesus to Paul so he could preach the Good News. Think about how God revealed Jesus to you and how you too might be able to share your faith with others.

FORGIVEN MUCH

Luke 7:36-8:3

[36] A Pharisee invited Jesus to have dinner with him, and Jesus went to his house and sat down to eat. [37] In that town was a woman who lived a sinful life. She heard that Jesus was eating in the Pharisee's house, so she brought an alabaster jar full of perfume [38] and stood behind Jesus, by his feet, crying and wetting his feet with her tears. Then she dried his feet with her hair, kissed them, and poured the perfume on them. [39] When the Pharisee saw this, he said to himself, "If this man really were a prophet, he would know who this woman is who is touching him; he would know what kind of sinful life she lives!"

[40] Jesus spoke up and said to him, "Simon, I have something to tell you."

"Yes, Teacher," he said, "tell me."

[41] "There were two men who owed money to a moneylender," Jesus began. "One owed him 500 silver coins, and the other owed him fifty. [42] Neither of them could pay him back, so he cancelled the debts of both. Which one, then, will love him more?"

[43] "I suppose," answered Simon, "that it would be the one who was forgiven more."

"You are right," said Jesus. [44] Then he turned to the woman and said to Simon, "Do you see this woman? I came into your home, and you gave me no water for my feet, but she has washed my feet with her tears and dried them with her hair. [45] You did not welcome me with a kiss, but she has not stopped kissing my feet since I came. [46] You provided no olive oil for my head, but she has covered my feet with perfume. [47] I tell you, then, the great love she has shown proves that her many sins have been forgiven. But whoever has been forgiven little shows only a little love."

[48] Then Jesus said to the woman, "Your sins are forgiven."

[49] The others sitting at the table began to say to themselves, "Who is this, who even forgives sins?"

[50] But Jesus said to the woman, "Your faith has saved you; go in peace."

[1] Some time later Jesus travelled through towns and villages, preaching the Good News about the Kingdom of God. The twelve disciples went with him, [2] and so did some women who had been healed of evil spirits and diseases: Mary (who was called Magdalene), from whom seven demons had been driven out; [3] Joanna, whose husband Chuza was an officer in Herod's court; and Susanna, and many other women who used their own resources to help Jesus and his disciples.

Other Readings: 2 Samuel 12:7-10, 13; Psalm 32:1-2, 5, 7, 11; Galatians 2:16, 19-21

LECTIO:

Jesus is invited for a meal by Simon the Pharisee. At that time, rich people would have eaten reclining on couches at a low table with their feet pointing away from the table.

A woman, probably a prostitute, washes Jesus' feet with her tears, dries them with her hair, kisses them and then anoints them with perfume. This would have been socially unacceptable. Simon judges them both, but judges Jesus even more than the woman because he did not stop her.

Jesus is fully aware what Simon is thinking. So he tells a parable about two people being forgiven debts they could not repay. Jesus makes the point that we are all sinners in need of forgiveness. The woman's actions show the sincerity of her repentance, her faith in Jesus, and love for him.

Luke then draws attention to the role of women in Jesus' ministry, naming three who travelled with him and the disciples while they preached the gospel. He also adds that many women supported Jesus' ministry from their own resources, probably with food and money.

 # MEDITATIO:

- In what way does Simon misjudge both Jesus and the woman?
- Consider the impact this encounter might have had on Simon, the other guests and the woman. What can we learn from this parable?
- Do you feel you have been forgiven much or just a little for your sins?

 # ORATIO:

Praise God, Jesus will cancel out our sins if we repent. Pray through the verses from Psalm 32. Ask the Holy Spirit to help you understand the real nature of grace.

 # CONTEMPLATIO:

Contemplate Jesus' sacrifice for you and God's gift of forgiveness. Consider what it means to live for God, not for yourself.

FORGETTING SELF

Luke 9:18-24

¹⁸ One day when Jesus was praying alone, the disciples came to him. "Who do the crowds say I am?" he asked them.

¹⁹ "Some say that you are John the Baptist," they answered. "Others say that you are Elijah, while others say that one of the prophets of long ago has come back to life."

²⁰ "What about you?" he asked them. "Who do you say I am?"

Peter answered, "You are God's Messiah."

²¹ Then Jesus gave them strict orders not to tell this to anyone. ²² He also said to them, "The Son of Man must suffer much and be rejected by the elders, the chief priests, and the teachers of the Law. He will be put to death, but three days later he will be raised to life."

²³ And he said to them all, "Anyone who wants to come with me must forget self, take up their cross every day, and follow me. ²⁴ For whoever wants to save their own life will lose it, but whoever loses their life for my sake will save it.

Other Readings: Zechariah 12:10-11, 13:1; Psalm 63:1-5, 7-8; Galatians 3:26-29

 LECTIO:

In this passage Jesus allows his disciples to know that he is indeed the Messiah. But he doesn't want this revealed publicly yet. He also starts to show them that he is a very different Messiah from the one they expected. In fact, he will be rejected by the very people who should have welcomed him most – the religious leaders. Even more shockingly he will be put to death. But three days later he will be raised back to life.

Jesus then talks about the cost of discipleship, 'Anyone who wants to come with me must forget self, take up their cross every day, and follow me' (verse 23). Jesus confronts the disciples with the tough reality. Being a Christian requires the daily choice of obeying God rather than following our own plans, even when this involves hardship and suffering. So whoever wants to be Jesus' disciple must be ready to give their life for their faith.

It must have seemed a frightening prospect to the disciples. But Jesus explains his first saying with the second, 'For whoever wants to save their own life will lose it, but whoever loses their life for my sake will save it'. So while ultimately following Jesus is the only way to save our life, sacrifice and suffering is part and parcel of the process.

These few words must have left the disciples reeling! While Jesus is indeed the Messiah, the idea of him being put to death rather than delivering the Jews victoriously from their Roman oppressors would have been shocking.

They must also have wondered what they had got involved in. Much of the Old Testament taught them that God blesses the righteous; it is those who disobey God that experience suffering. Where would following Jesus lead them?

Following Jesus involves putting his will and kingdom first whatever the cost or consequences to us personally.

 # MEDITATIO:

- Today and throughout history people have had very different ideas about Jesus. Who do you think he is?
- Consider how Jesus unites the idea of a suffering Messiah with that of a suffering disciple. How do you respond to suffering in your life?
- What does it mean in practical terms for you to lose your life and take up your cross daily? In which areas of your life do you find it hardest to do what God wants rather than what you want?

 # ORATIO:

Read through today's responsorial Psalm several times. Do these verses express how you feel? Use them for an honest conversation with God. What strikes you most? Maybe God wants you to bring it to him in prayer.

 # CONTEMPLATIO:

Sit and contemplate a crucifix for a while each day this week. Think about all it symbolises and its relevance for you each day. What does Jesus' death and resurrection change?

FOLLOW ME

Luke 9:51-62

⁵¹ As the time drew near when Jesus would be taken up to heaven, he made up his mind and set out on his way to Jerusalem. ⁵² He sent messengers ahead of him, who went into a village in Samaria to get everything ready for him. ⁵³ But the people there would not receive him, because it was clear that he was on his way to Jerusalem. ⁵⁴ When the disciples James and John saw this, they said, "Lord, do you want us to call fire down from heaven to destroy them?"

⁵⁵ Jesus turned and rebuked them. ⁵⁶ Then Jesus and his disciples went on to another village.

⁵⁷ As they went on their way, a man said to Jesus, "I will follow you wherever you go."

⁵⁸ Jesus said to him, "Foxes have holes, and birds have nests, but the Son of Man has nowhere to lie down and rest."

⁵⁹ He said to another man, "Follow me."

But that man said, "Sir, first let me go back and bury my father."

⁶⁰ Jesus answered, "Let the dead bury their own dead. You go and proclaim the Kingdom of God."

⁶¹ Someone else said, "I will follow you, sir; but first let me go and say goodbye to my family."

⁶² Jesus said to him, "Anyone who starts to plough and then keeps looking back is of no use to the Kingdom of God."

Other Readings: 1 Kings 19:16, 19-21; Psalm 16:1-2, 5, 7-11; Galatians 5:1, 13-18

 LECTIO:

Jesus needs a bed for the night in a certain Samaritan village. When the Samaritans realise Jesus is heading for Jerusalem, they turn him away.

There was centuries of friction between Jews and Samaritans. Many Jews regarded Samaritans as worse than pagans and tried to avoid any contact with them.

James and John react strongly when the Samaritans turn Jesus away and want to call down God's judgement to destroy them. But Jesus rebukes his disciples for their response and simply moves on.

Next Luke tells us about a series of encounters with people who seem to be keen to become Jesus' disciples. Jesus is on his way to die for the sake of the gospel and is looking for total commitment in those who want to be his disciples. So he is direct and tests their sincerity.

In the first exchange Jesus says '...the Son of Man has nowhere to lie down and rest.' This is a reminder that ultimately Jesus' home is not in this world. The same is true for Christians - 'We, however, are citizens of heaven,' (Philippians 3:20).

Another man wants to follow Jesus but first he asks to bury his father. At face value this seems a reasonable request. Jesus' reply seems harsh and uncaring. We know Jesus upholds honouring one's parents. Following Jesus must be our first priority. Taking care of family obligations must be out of obedience to Jesus, not an excuse for delaying obedience to him.

The same idea is expressed in verses 61-62. To plough a straight furrow you need to stay focused on the task in front of you. If you keep looking back you will veer off course.

As we learned last week there is no quick fix for disciples. Jesus must come first and following him costs everything.

 # MEDITATIO:

- How do the ideas contained here challenge your own priorities? Have you ever said to Jesus, 'yes, but later...'?
- In what ways can we 'proclaim the Kingdom of God'?
- Consider Jesus' attitude to John and James after their emotional outburst against the Samaritans. What can we learn from this?

 # ORATIO:

Ask God to speak to you from today's passage. Tell him honestly how you feel about it.

If you really want to be one of his disciples, ask the Holy Spirit to help you with the areas of your life you find hardest to give to God. Ask God to help you focus on serving him and not get distracted by things that take you off course.

 # CONTEMPLATIO:

Consider the Kingdom of God. What influence does it have on your life? Consider what it really means to follow Jesus and be his disciple.

DIVINE HELP

John 14:15-16, 23-26

[15] "If you love me, you will obey my commandments. [16] I will ask the Father, and he will give you another Helper, who will stay with you for ever.

[23] Jesus answered him, "Whoever loves me will obey my teaching. My Father will love him, and my Father and I will come to him and live with him. [24] Whoever does not love me does not obey my teaching. And the teaching you have heard is not mine, but comes from the Father, who sent me.

[25] "I have told you this while I am still with you. [26] The Helper, the Holy Spirit, whom the Father will send in my name, will teach you everything and make you remember all that I have told you.

Other Readings: Acts 2:1-11; Psalm 104:1, 24, 29-31, 34; Romans 8:8-17

 LECTIO:

We return to the gospel passage we read two weeks ago along with verses 15-16 from earlier in the chapter. This teaching is so important that Jesus repeats it to help his first disciples remember it and put it into practice. Today we too have another opportunity to consider the significance of Jesus' words.

Jesus asks the disciples to love him. Easy enough to say 'yes', you might think. But Jesus makes it clear that loving him takes far more than a simple word. Love in Jesus eyes has a very practical outcome and it takes the shape of obedience to his commandments.

Jesus continues with an amazing promise for everyone who obeys him. Both the Father and Jesus will come and live with them. Jesus does not explain exactly what this 'living with' will be like but it surely indicates a very special and intimate personal relationship.

At this point Jesus makes it clear that these words are not his own idea. This teaching comes directly from God the Father, which is of course equally true of all Jesus' words.

Jesus now talks about the helper, who he reveals as the Holy Spirit. Sometimes the Holy Spirit is overlooked as people deepen their relationships with Jesus and the Father. But he plays a huge part in our relationship with Jesus. In this reading he is revealed to be a teacher and helper for the disciples, reminding them of Jesus' teaching and helping them to understand and live it.

Perhaps in another sense the Holy Spirit is Jesus' helper too. He continues the work Jesus started in the lives of the first disciples and in us today, now that Jesus has returned to his Father.

Jesus also repeats to the disciples that he will ask the Father to send the Holy Spirit to help them after he returns to heaven and promises that the Holy Spirit will stay with them forever.

 MEDITATIO:

- Consider the role of God the Father in this passage.
- Which words of Jesus strike you most from today's readings?
- How do you respond to this connection between love and obedience?
- Do you find some areas of Jesus' teaching difficult to obey and put into practice in your life? What can you do about this?
- Consider the importance of the Holy Spirit in your everyday life. Read Romans 8:1-17. Think about what this means for you.

 ORATIO:

Today we remember the dramatic way the Holy Spirit filled the first disciples on the day of Pentecost. Prayerfully read Acts 2:1-11 and give thanks to God for sending us the Holy Spirit to be our helper.

Each day this week, ask the Holy Spirit to fill you afresh and help you to live in a way that will please Jesus. It's only with the Holy Spirit's help that we can obediently love and serve Jesus.

 CONTEMPLATIO:

'For the Spirit that God has given you does not make you slaves and cause you to be afraid; instead, the Spirit makes you God's children, and by the Spirit's power we cry out to God, Father! My Father!' Romans 8:15

Consider what an incredible privilege it is to be able to call Almighty God our Father and what it means to be his children.

LOVE IN ACTION

Luke 10:25-37

²⁵ A teacher of the Law came up and tried to trap Jesus. "Teacher," he asked, "what must I do to receive eternal life?"

²⁶ Jesus answered him, "What do the Scriptures say? How do you interpret them?"

²⁷ The man answered, " 'Love the Lord your God with all your heart, with all your soul, with all your strength, and with all your mind'; and 'Love your neighbour as you love yourself.' "

²⁸ "You are right," Jesus replied; "do this and you will live."

²⁹ But the teacher of the Law wanted to justify himself, so he asked Jesus, "Who is my neighbour?"

³⁰ Jesus answered, "There was once a man who was going down from Jerusalem to Jericho when robbers attacked him, stripped him, and beat him up, leaving him half dead. ³¹ It so happened that a priest was going down that road; but when he saw the man, he walked on by, on the other side. ³² In the same way a Levite also came along, went over and looked at the man, and then walked on by, on the other side. ³³ But a Samaritan who was travelling that way came upon the man, and when he saw him, his heart was filled with pity. ³⁴ He went over to him, poured oil and wine on his wounds and bandaged them; then he put the man on his own animal and took him to an inn, where he took care of him. ³⁵ The next day he took out two silver coins and gave them to the innkeeper. 'Take care of him,' he told the innkeeper, 'and when I come back this way, I will pay you whatever else you spend on him.' "

³⁶ And Jesus concluded, "In your opinion, which one of these three acted like a neighbour towards the man attacked by the robbers?"

³⁷ The teacher of the Law answered, "The one who was kind to him."

Jesus replied, "You go, then, and do the same."

Other Readings: Deuteronomy 30:10-14; Psalm 69:13, 16, 29-30, 32-33, 35-36; Colossians 1:15-20

 LECTIO:

A teacher wants to trap Jesus with a question. Jesus sees straight through him and asks him to answer his own question. The teacher gives the correct answer that sums up the Jewish teaching: loving God and loving our neighbour.

But the teacher hasn't achieved his objective of making himself look cleverer than Jesus so he asks another question, "Who is my neighbour?" Jesus responds with a powerful parable – the Good Samaritan, as we know it today.

Jesus contrasts the responses of three people when they encounter a man at the side of the road who has been robbed and beaten up. The first two, a priest and a Levite were in positions of religious authority. They would have sought to obey the law in every detail but here they fail to obey one of the most important commandments.

It is the third person, a Samaritan, who acts like a good neighbour and helps this man. To appreciate the full impact of this parable we need to understand the longstanding animosity that existed here. The Jews looked down on the Samaritans and considered them 'unclean', no better than Gentiles. Jesus uses a non-Jew, a despised foreigner, to show this religious teacher how to live out Jewish teaching!

With this parable Jesus makes it clear that we should always be neighbours to any fellow human being who needs help. We may never have met them before, they may be from a different racial and religious background, but nonetheless we are still their neighbours.

 # MEDITATIO:

- Consider the reasons the priest and the Levite might have had for not helping the man. Do you see any of these attitudes in yourself? What needs to motivate our actions towards others?
- What do we learn from this passage about why we should help others in need?
- Is it significant that Jesus says 'do this' (verses 28 and 37)? What light does James 2:14-17 shed on this?
- Think about what it means for you to love God with all your heart, soul, strength and mind.

 # ORATIO:

Let Psalm 69 guide your prayers for those you love and for those you see in need.

 # CONTEMPLATIO:

Read Colossians 1:15-20 slowly several times. Then take a couple of lines at a time and contemplate the meaning of the magnificence of Christ revealed here.

TRUSTING JESUS

John 14:23-29

[23] Jesus answered him, "Whoever loves me will obey my teaching. My Father will love him, and my Father and I will come to him and live with him. [24] Whoever does not love me does not obey my teaching. And the teaching you have heard is not mine, but comes from the Father, who sent me.

[25] "I have told you this while I am still with you. [26] The Helper, the Holy Spirit, whom the Father will send in my name, will teach you everything and make you remember all that I have told you.

[27] "Peace is what I leave with you; it is my own peace that I give you. I do not give it as the world does. Do not be worried and upset; do not be afraid. [28] You heard me say to you, 'I am leaving, but I will come back to you.' If you loved me, you would be glad that I am going to the Father; for he is greater than I. [29] I have told you this now before it all happens, so that when it does happen, you will believe.

Other Readings: Acts 15:1-2, 22-29; Psalm 67:1-2, 4-5, 7; Revelation 21:10-14, 22-23

 LECTIO:

This week we continue to read about the teaching Jesus gave to his disciples in the context of the Last Supper (John 14-17). Today's text is a response to a question from another disciple called Judas. (John 13:31-35 makes it clear this is not Judas Iscariot as he had left them earlier to betray Jesus.)

Jesus has just said that he will reveal himself to those who love him (verse 21). Judas is puzzled. Is Jesus saying he will only reveal himself to the disciples? Jesus doesn't answer Judas directly even though it is apparent his understanding is very limited. Jesus knows the disciples will get more insight after his resurrection. So for now he emphasises again his relationship to God the Father. He stresses that his teaching comes direct from the Father and that the critical point is for each one to put his teaching into action.

But Jesus makes it plain he doesn't expect us to be able to do this on our own. God the Father is going to send us a helper. The Holy Spirit is going to teach us everything we need to know to live, love and serve Jesus.

Jesus tells them he will be leaving them to go to the Father. He doesn't reveal just how soon this will be or explain the shocking nature of his death. But he does seek to reassure them. He promises them he will come back for them, that they won't be left on their own but will have the Holy Spirit to help them and he leaves his peace with them.

Jesus wants them to trust him. Even though they don't understand everything now, later they will see what he was saying and believe in him.

 # MEDITATIO:

- Why does Jesus put so much emphasis on living out the gospel message to express your love for him?
- How easy do you find it to trust God when you don't get the answers you expect or you don't understand things? What can we learn from this passage to help us?
- How do you relate to the Holy Spirit? Do you ask for his help to put Jesus' teaching into practice in your life?
- How does Jesus leave us his peace?

 # ORATIO:

Thank God for sending Jesus and the Holy Spirit. Ask God to speak to you and show you how he wants you to respond to him today. This may be out of a word or phrase from the Scripture passage or it maybe something prompted by one of the questions above. Take your time.

 # CONTEMPLATIO:

Think about how much God loves you and how he has shown his love for you. Marvel at the wonderful promise that the Father and Jesus come to live with us.

PRAY LIKE JESUS

Luke 11:1-13

¹ One day Jesus was praying in a certain place. When he had finished, one of his disciples said to him, "Lord, teach us to pray, just as John taught his disciples."

² Jesus said to them, "When you pray, say this:

'Father:

 May your holy name be honoured;

 may your Kingdom come.

³ Give us day by day the food we need.

⁴ Forgive us our sins,

 for we forgive everyone who does us wrong.

 And do not bring us to hard testing.' "

⁵ And Jesus said to his disciples, "Suppose one of you should go to a friend's house at midnight and say, 'Friend, let me borrow three loaves of bread. ⁶ A friend of mine who is on a journey has just come to my house, and I haven't got any food for him!' ⁷ And suppose your friend should answer from inside, 'Don't bother me! The door is already locked, and my children and I are in bed. I can't get up and give you anything.' ⁸ Well, what then? I tell you that even if he will not get up and give you the bread because you are his friend, yet he will get up and give you everything you need because you are not ashamed to keep on asking.

⁹ "And so I say to you: ask, and you will receive; seek, and you will find; knock, and the door will be opened to you. ¹⁰ For all those who ask will receive, and those who seek will find, and the door will be opened to anyone who knocks. ¹¹ Would any of you who are fathers give your son a snake when he asks for fish? ¹² Or would you give him a scorpion when he asks for an egg? ¹³ Bad as you are, you know how to give good things to your children. How much more, then, will the Father in heaven give the Holy Spirit to those who ask him!"

Other Readings: Genesis 18:20-32; Psalm 138:1-3, 6-8; Colossians 2:12-14

 LECTIO:

Prayer is at the heart of today's teaching. The disciples felt their prayers were not up to the mark and asked Jesus to give them some guidance. There are two versions of the Lord's prayer, this one from Luke and Matthew's version (Matthew 6: 9-13). Matthew's version is longer and better known by Christians as it is used in the liturgy.

Jesus keeps the prayer guide short and simple. Most importantly he wants the disciples to recognise it's a relationship between Father and child.

The first step is to acknowledge God as our Father recognising his holiness and honouring him. Next we should pray for his Kingdom rule to come. Then we can make any essential requests, for example food for the day, forgiveness of our sins and protection from hard testing.

Jesus didn't intend us to only pray these exact words. Rather they provide us with a framework and guidance on the type of things we should pray about.

The only thing that is subject to any condition is forgiveness. If we do not forgive those who sin against us, then we won't receive forgiveness ourselves.

Jesus goes on to teach about the importance of being persistent in prayer and concludes with the illustration of a father and son. Most human fathers give good things to their children rather than things that are harmful. How much more then will our heavenly father, who knows us perfectly, give us what we need? Of course, sometimes this may mean God not giving us what we ask for because he knows it would be harmful for us.

 MEDITATIO:

- What does this passage reveal to us about God and how he wants us to approach him?
- How do you feel about God being your Father?
- How does the condition of forgiving others in order to receive your own forgiveness affect you?
- What is your own experience of prayer? What can you learn from this passage to help you?

 ORATIO:

Pray through these verses from the Lord's prayer. After each line add your own words. Ask the Holy Spirit to help and guide you. Take your time.

 CONTEMPLATIO:

Consider today's responsorial verse Psalm 138:3:
  'You answered me when I called to you;
  With your strength you strengthened me.'

FORGETTING SELF

Luke 9:18-24

¹⁸ One day when Jesus was praying alone, the disciples came to him. "Who do the crowds say I am?" he asked them.

¹⁹ "Some say that you are John the Baptist," they answered. "Others say that you are Elijah, while others say that one of the prophets of long ago has come back to life."

²⁰ "What about you?" he asked them. "Who do you say I am?"

Peter answered, "You are God's Messiah."

²¹ Then Jesus gave them strict orders not to tell this to anyone. ²² He also said to them, "The Son of Man must suffer much and be rejected by the elders, the chief priests, and the teachers of the Law. He will be put to death, but three days later he will be raised to life."

²³ And he said to them all, "Anyone who wants to come with me must forget self, take up their cross every day, and follow me. ²⁴ For whoever wants to save their own life will lose it, but whoever loses their life for my sake will save it.

Other Readings: Zechariah 12:10-11, 13:1; Psalm 63:1-5, 7-8; Galatians 3:26-29

 LECTIO:

In this passage Jesus allows his disciples to know that he is indeed the Messiah. But he doesn't want this revealed publicly yet. He also starts to show them that he is a very different Messiah from the one they expected. In fact, he will be rejected by the very people who should have welcomed him most – the religious leaders. Even more shockingly he will be put to death. But three days later he will be raised back to life.

Jesus then talks about the cost of discipleship, 'Anyone who wants to come with me must forget self, take up their cross every day, and follow me' (verse 23). Jesus confronts the disciples with the tough reality. Being a Christian requires the daily choice of obeying God rather than following our own plans, even when this involves hardship and suffering. So whoever wants to be Jesus' disciple must be ready to give their life for their faith.

It must have seemed a frightening prospect to the disciples. But Jesus explains his first saying with the second, 'For whoever wants to save their own life will lose it, but whoever loses their life for my sake will save it'. So while ultimately following Jesus is the only way to save our life, sacrifice and suffering is part and parcel of the process.

These few words must have left the disciples reeling! While Jesus is indeed the Messiah, the idea of him being put to death rather than delivering the Jews victoriously from their Roman oppressors would have been shocking.

They must also have wondered what they had got involved in. Much of the Old Testament taught them that God blesses the righteous; it is those who disobey God that experience suffering. Where would following Jesus lead them?

Following Jesus involves putting his will and kingdom first whatever the cost or consequences to us personally.

 # MEDITATIO:

- Today and throughout history people have had very different ideas about Jesus. Who do you think he is?
- Consider how Jesus unites the idea of a suffering Messiah with that of a suffering disciple. How do you respond to suffering in your life?
- What does it mean in practical terms for you to lose your life and take up your cross daily? In which areas of your life do you find it hardest to do what God wants rather than what you want?

 # ORATIO:

Read through today's responsorial Psalm several times. Do these verses express how you feel? Use them for an honest conversation with God. What strikes you most? Maybe God wants you to bring it to him in prayer.

 # CONTEMPLATIO:

Sit and contemplate a crucifix for a while each day this week. Think about all it symbolises and its relevance for you each day. What does Jesus' death and resurrection change?

HEAVENLY PRIORITIES

Luke 12:32-48

32 "Do not be afraid, little flock, for your Father is pleased to give you the Kingdom. 33 Sell all your belongings and give the money to the poor. Provide for yourselves purses that don't wear out, and save your riches in heaven, where they will never decrease, because no thief can get to them, and no moth can destroy them. 34 For your heart will always be where your riches are.

35 "Be ready for whatever comes, dressed for action and with your lamps lit, 36 like servants who are waiting for their master to come back from a wedding feast. When he comes and knocks, they will open the door for him at once. 37 How happy are those servants whose master finds them awake and ready when he returns! I tell you, he will take off his coat, ask them to sit down, and will wait on them. 38 How happy they are if he finds them ready, even if he should come at midnight or even later! 39 And you can be sure that if the owner of a house knew the time when the thief would come, he would not let the thief break into his house. 40 And you, too, must be ready, because the Son of Man will come at an hour when you are not expecting him."

41 Peter said, "Lord, does this parable apply to us, or do you mean it for everyone?"

42 The Lord answered, "Who, then, is the faithful and wise servant? He is the one that his master will put in charge, to run the household and give the other servants their share of the food at the proper time. 43 How happy that servant is if his master finds him doing this when he comes home! 44 Indeed, I tell you, the master will put that servant in charge of all his property. 45 But if that servant says to himself that his master is taking a long time to come back and if he begins to beat the other servants, both the men and the women, and eats and drinks and gets drunk, 46 then the master will come back one day when the servant does not expect him and at a time he does not know. The master will cut him in pieces and make him share the fate of the disobedient.

47 "The servant who knows what his master wants him to do, but does not get himself ready and do it, will be punished with a heavy whipping. 48 But the servant who does not know what his master wants, and yet does something for which he deserves a whipping, will be punished with a light whipping. Much is required from the person to whom much is given; much more is required from the person to whom much more is given.

Other Readings: Wisdom 18:6-9; Psalm 33:1, 12, 18-20, 22; Hebrews 11:1-2, 8-19

LECTIO:

The essence of what Jesus is saying here is summed up in two simple ideas. Make sure you are storing up your riches in the right place – heaven – and be prepared for Jesus' return.

Luke reminds us of the totality of God's provision for us through all time. In these uncertain days we can be confident our heavenly father will provide for us. So we can freely share our worldly goods knowing God recognises every investment of trust we make in him and will also supply our needs from his heavenly treasure house.

Many Christians in Luke's day expected Jesus to return at any moment. Luke reminds us to be ready no matter how long the wait. God's timetable will not be revealed to us in advance, the timing of Jesus' return will be a surprise.

 # MEDITATIO:

- Consider Jesus' words in verse 32. As Christians we can feel in the minority. Draw strength from living in God's kingdom.
- Make a list of all the things that are most important to you at this point in your life – your 'riches'. Consider where these 'riches' are invested?
- How do you maintain a state of readiness for Jesus to return?

 # ORATIO:

Ask God to speak to you from today's Gospel reading. Maybe he will have something to say about your 'riches' or how to be more prepared for his return.

 # CONTEMPLATIO:

After reading Hebrews 11, consider what sustained these believers and allow God to show you how he can sustain you too.

GOD COMES TO SAVE

Luke 7:11-17

[11] Soon afterwards Jesus went to a town called Nain, accompanied by his disciples and a large crowd. [12] Just as he arrived at the gate of the town, a funeral procession was coming out. The dead man was the only son of a woman who was a widow, and a large crowd from the town was with her. [13] When the Lord saw her, his heart was filled with pity for her, and he said to her, "Don't cry." [14] Then he walked over and touched the coffin, and the men carrying it stopped. Jesus said, "Young man! Get up, I tell you!" [15] The dead man sat up and began to talk, and Jesus gave him back to his mother.

[16] They all were filled with fear and praised God. "A great prophet has appeared among us!" they said; "God has come to save his people!"

[17] This news about Jesus went out through all the country and the surrounding territory.

Other Readings: 1 Kings 17:17-24; Psalm 30:1, 3-5, 10-12; Galatians 1:11-19

 LECTIO:

Can you imagine this scene in a small town near Nazareth? A large crowd, women wailing and a funeral procession is passing by. The chief mourner is an older woman.

This poor woman has already lost her husband. Now her only child is dead and all her future security has died with him. She is left behind with no one to provide for even her most basic needs. Her grief is pain-filled and raw.

Jesus joins the sympathetic crowd. No one asks him to intervene but compassion moves him to act. He touches the makeshift coffin, probably no more than a plank used to carry the dead body for burial.

This tiny action made Jesus ceremonially unclean and would have shocked those around him. The procession comes to a halt. Jesus tells the dead body to get up. The young man sits up and starts to talk! Jesus 'gives him back to his mother'. Luke repeats this exact phrase from 1 Kings 17:23 describing the miraculous raising of another widow's son – this time by Elijah.

The people don't know who to look at first - the man raised back to life, his ecstatic mother or Jesus, who right in front of their very eyes has repeated the miracle performed by one of their greatest prophets, Elijah.

Fear and praise grip the crowd at the same time. They echo the words of Zechariah's prophecy about the Messiah (Luke 1:67-75), 'God has come to save his people!'

This event takes on added significance when seen in context. Read the verses before and after it in Luke 7. This miracle follows straight after the healing of the Roman officer's servant, when Jesus was amazed at the officer's great faith. Jesus demonstrated his authority over sickness and the servant was healed.

In the verses after today's Gospel reading two of John the Baptist's disciples arrive. They have been sent by John to establish if Jesus is the long-awaited Messiah. Jesus simply tells them to report what is happening – people are being healed, the dead raised and the gospel is being preached. Jesus knew John would make the connection with the Messianic prophecies he was fulfilling such as Isaiah 35:5.

 # MEDITATIO:

- Imagine you were one of the mourners that witnessed this once in a lifetime miracle. What would you have thought about Jesus after seeing this miracle?
- The verses that precede today's reading highlight Jesus' authority over sickness. This miracle demonstrates that Jesus has authority over death. Why is this significant?

 # ORATIO:

The widow didn't ask Jesus to help her but he chose to intervene. Think about the times Jesus has intervened in your life to help you. Take some time to express your thanks and praise to God.

The Psalmist gives his testimony in Psalm 30. Let these words inspire your prayers too.

 # CONTEMPLATIO:

In Galatians 1:11-19 we read how God revealed Jesus to Paul so he could preach the Good News. Think about how God revealed Jesus to you and how you too might be able to share your faith with others.

THE NARROW DOOR

Luke 13:22-30

²² Jesus went through towns and villages, teaching the people and making his way towards Jerusalem. ²³ Someone asked him, "Sir, will just a few people be saved?"

Jesus answered them, ²⁴ "Do your best to go in through the narrow door; because many people will surely try to go in but will not be able. ²⁵ The master of the house will get up and close the door; then when you stand outside and begin to knock on the door and say, 'Open the door for us, sir!' he will answer you, 'I don't know where you come from!' ²⁶ Then you will answer, 'We ate and drank with you; you taught in our town!' ²⁷ But he will say again, 'I don't know where you come from. Get away from me, all you wicked people!' ²⁸ How you will cry and grind your teeth when you see Abraham, Isaac, and Jacob, and all the prophets in the Kingdom of God, while you are thrown out! ²⁹ People will come from the east and the west, from the north and the south, and sit down at the feast in the Kingdom of God. ³⁰ Then those who are now last will be first, and those who are now first will be last."

Other Readings: Isaiah 66:18-21; Psalm 117; Hebrews 12:5-7, 11-13

 LECTIO:

Life as a Christian demands a lot of the believer. Today Jesus talks about who will and who won't be allowed into the Kingdom of God. He warns his listeners both then and now to do more than just listen to his teaching.

Sadly, if you are not actively allowing Jesus to impact your everyday life you are not really living as a Christian at all. Christian living involves more than just attending church – it's all to do with your personal relationship with God through Jesus.

For some people, listening to Jesus' teaching became an intellectual exercise. They treated Jesus as just another rabbi, asking theoretical questions like the one in verse 23, and taking it for granted they'd be saved.

Jesus warns them they are in serious danger of losing their chance to enter the Kingdom of God. He compares it to a house with a very small entrance. People are struggling to get in but the owner has closed the door and is only allowing certain people to enter.

Jesus is making his meaning very clear. There has to be a personal entering in to faith in God by believing in Jesus and then a practical application of faith to every part of your life.

Jesus is reminding us there can be no sitting on a fence in matters of faith. If you belong to him, his teaching will impact your life. You may make mistakes but you will be endeavouring to live your life in obedience to him. Anyone who does not repent and choose this option is risking everything, as the day may come when the 'house owner' does not recognise you and allow you to enter in.

 # MEDITATIO:

- The narrow door refers to a time when an individual repents and makes a personal commitment of faith in God through Jesus. It is not something someone else can do for you as it requires a personal choice. Can you remember the time when you made the choice to follow Jesus? For some people it can be a gradual process taking years. For others there was a special day when they took the decision. If you are not sure, why not talk about it with your priest or minister?

 # ORATIO:

'Keep on working with fear and trembling to complete your salvation, because God is always at work in you to make you willing and able to obey his own purpose. (Philippians 2:12-13)

In these verses the Apostle Paul exhorts the Philippian believers not to be complacent but to continue their life of faith. Ask the Holy Spirit to make you willing and able to obey God's purposes for your life.

 # CONTEMPLATIO:

The reading from Philippians reminds us that God is at work in each one of us. Consider the ways God is working in your life right now. He may show you some ways that surprise you.

WALK HUMBLY

Luke 14:1, 7-14

¹ One Sabbath Jesus went to eat a meal at the home of one of the leading Pharisees; and people were watching Jesus closely.

⁷ Jesus noticed how some of the guests were choosing the best places, so he told this parable to all of them: ⁸ "When someone invites you to a wedding feast, do not sit down in the best place. It could happen that someone more important than you has been invited, ⁹ and your host, who invited both of you, would have to come and say to you, 'Let him have this place.' Then you would be embarrassed and have to sit in the lowest place. ¹⁰ Instead, when you are invited, go and sit in the lowest place, so that your host will come to you and say, 'Come on up, my friend, to a better place.' This will bring you honour in the presence of all the other guests. ¹¹ For all those who make themselves great will be humbled, and those who humble themselves will be made great."

¹² Then Jesus said to his host, "When you give a lunch or a dinner, do not invite your friends or your brothers or your relatives or your rich neighbours – for they will invite you back, and in this way you will be paid for what you did. ¹³ When you give a feast, invite the poor, the crippled, the lame, and the blind; ¹⁴ and you will be blessed, because they are not able to pay you back. God will repay you on the day the good people rise from death."

Other Readings: Ecclesiasticus 3:17-20, 28-29; Psalm 68:3-6, 9-10; Hebrews 12:18-19, 22-24

 LECTIO:

Today we join Jesus as he dines with a leading Pharisee. All the guests at the dinner are watching to see how Jesus will behave. What they don't notice is Jesus observing their proud ways.

In Jesus' day the most important seats were close to the host and each of the Pharisees' guests wanted one of these seats for themselves.

Jesus uses the opportunity to teach the dinner guests a better way to behave. His comments are a reminder of Jewish teaching summed up in verses like Proverbs 25:6-7, "When you stand before the king, don't try to impress him and pretend to be important. It is better to be asked to take a higher position than to be told to give your place to someone more important."

Of course the irony is that had the host realised who Jesus was then he would have immediately given Jesus the place of honour.

Jesus then emphasises hospitality and generosity towards people who cannot reciprocate - the poor and physically disadvantaged. Again it is a question of our attitudes. Do we exclude others because of selfishness or pride?

Jesus' concern is always to be inclusive. He spent time with people who were not considered 'respectable'. The Kingdom of God should be, and is, open to all irrespective of man-made social status because before God we are all sinners in need of salvation.

MEDITATIO:

- The apostle Peter took Jesus' words to heart as he also taught, 'And all of you must put on the apron of humility, to serve one another; for the scripture says, "God resists the proud but shows favour to the humble." Humble yourselves, then, under God's mighty hand, so that he will lift you up in his own good time'. (1 Peter 5:5-6)
- Jesus regularly reminded his listeners about humility. Why do you think it is so important for us to keep a humble attitude towards others? Why is pride so dangerous?
- Think about who you invite to your home. Does Jesus' teaching challenge your choice of guests?

ORATIO:

Ask God to speak to you from today's reading about humility and hospitality.

Read Psalm 68:1-10. Notice the contrast between God's majesty and his concern for the poor, the lonely, for widows, orphans and prisoners. Pray for people in these situations. The Holy Spirit may bring specific people to mind. God may also show you something practical you can do to help.

CONTEMPLATIO:

Read Philippians 2:3-11 and think about the example Jesus gives us of humility and service. Let God bring to mind small steps you can take in this direction during the coming weeks.

DEMANDS OF DISCIPLESHIP

Luke 14:25-33

[25] Once when large crowds of people were going along with Jesus, he turned and said to them, [26] "Those who come to me cannot be my disciples unless they love me more than they love father and mother, wife and children, brothers and sisters, and themselves as well. [27] Those who do not carry their own cross and come after me cannot be my disciples.

[28] "If one of you is planning to build a tower, you sit down first and work out what it will cost, to see if you have enough money to finish the job. [29] If you don't, you will not be able to finish the tower after laying the foundation; and all who see what happened will laugh at you. [30] 'This man began to build but can't finish the job!' they will say.

[31] "If a king goes out with 10,000 men to fight another king who comes against him with 20,000 men, he will sit down first and decide if he is strong enough to face that other king. [32] If he isn't, he will send messengers to meet the other king, to ask for terms of peace while he is still a long way off. [33] In the same way," concluded Jesus, "none of you can be my disciple unless you give up everything you have."

Other Readings: Wisdom 9:13-18; Psalm 90:3-6, 12-14, 17; Philemon 9-10, 12-17

 LECTIO:

Jesus is talking to the crowds around him about the challenges discipleship will bring. Many are following him just because he is a popular teacher. But the disciples also knew that trouble follows close behind Jesus. They were already experiencing a level of persecution from the religious authorities.

In any relationship there comes a time when you must decide whether to get serious about it or not. And that's exactly what Jesus is talking about today. The Christian life is not for those seeking popularity or a good time with no responsibilities.

As Jesus explains the position it becomes more challenging. Things that seem good can damage our heavenly relationship. Jesus tells us to think again. Nothing must hinder our relationship with him. So Mum and Dad, husband or wife, our children and our own needs and desires must take second place to Jesus' will. This is how Jesus' relationship with his beloved father worked.

Shockingly, we have to be willing to surrender our lives to the extent of being crucified in some way. This is painful stuff. Our calling is to do Jesus' will no matter the suffering or humiliation it brings. Our selfish ways must submit to God's will. This sort of living touches every area of life and gradually brings it into line with Jesus. And it costs us everything.

For this reason Jesus uses strong and graphic images to make us consider the cost before we start the discipleship journey.

In John 6:43-71 the crowds were horrified by some aspects of Jesus' teaching and many left him. Jesus makes it clear that humanly speaking it is impossible to follow him. It is only possible by God's Spirit. And in John 6:65 Jesus says 'no one can come to me unless the Father makes it possible for him to do so'.

 # MEDITATIO:

- What impacts you most from reading these verses? Is there a specific aspect of your life that seems at odds with Jesus' teaching?

 # ORATIO:

Humbly spend some time with God. Ask him to help you submit everything in your life to him. Ask the Holy Spirit to give you the strength and grace to follow Jesus no matter what the consequences. Keep your eyes fixed on Jesus. 1 Thessalonians 5:23-24 offers us great encouragement:

> 'May the God who gives us peace make you holy in every way and keep your whole being – spirit, soul and body – free from every fault at the coming of our Lord Jesus Christ. He who calls you will do it, because he is faithful.'

 # CONTEMPLATIO:

Think about the example Jesus himself gives us of living a life completely submitted to God. He also knew his father's total love for him.

Consider the suffering Jesus endured on the cross so that we can live a life free from sin and pleasing to God.

JOY IN HEAVEN

Luke 15:1-10

¹ One day when many tax collectors and other outcasts came to listen to Jesus, ² the Pharisees and the teachers of the Law started grumbling, "This man welcomes outcasts and even eats with them!" ³ So Jesus told them this parable:

⁴ "Suppose one of you has a hundred sheep and loses one of them – what do you do? You leave the other ninety-nine sheep in the pasture and go looking for the one that got lost until you find it. ⁵ When you find it, you are so happy that you put it on your shoulders ⁶ and carry it back home. Then you call your friends and neighbours together and say to them, 'I am so happy I found my lost sheep. Let us celebrate!' ⁷ In the same way, I tell you, there will be more joy in heaven over one sinner who repents than over ninety-nine respectable people who do not need to repent.

⁸ "Or suppose a woman who has ten silver coins loses one of them – what does she do? She lights a lamp, sweeps her house, and looks carefully everywhere until she finds it. ⁹ When she finds it, she calls her friends and neighbours together, and says to them, 'I am so happy I found the coin I lost. Let us celebrate!' ¹⁰ In the same way, I tell you, the angels of God rejoice over one sinner who repents."

This is the shorter form reading. The full Gospel reading continues with the parable of the Lost or Prodigal Son, Luke 15:11-32. We looked at these verses on the Fourth Sunday of Lent.

Other Readings: Exodus 32:7-11, 13-14; Psalm 51:1-2, 10-11, 15, 17; 1 Timothy 1:12-17

 LECTIO:

Once again the 'authorities' are outraged. Luke tells us the Jewish religious leaders criticised Jesus for his friendly attitude to 'sinners'.

Tax collectors topped the 'sinner list'. They were hated by the Jews because they took money for the pagan occupiers, the Romans. In fact one of Jesus' own disciples was once a tax collector - Levi, traditionally thought to be Matthew (Mark 2: 13-17).

In Luke 15 Jesus tells the Pharisees three parables: the lost sheep, the lost coin and the lost son.

The parable of the lost sheep underlines how far the shepherd will go to find just one missing sheep from his flock and his great joy when the lost sheep is found and returned to his care and protection.

The parable of the lost coin reinforces the point. Again, something of value is lost. The woman searches everywhere until she finds it. The fact that she still has nine other coins doesn't matter. One is lost and must be found.

Both the shepherd and the woman are filled with joy when what was lost is restored to them. Similarly all heaven rejoices when a sinner repents - a broken relationship is restored.

The lost or prodigal son is the third parable. The lost son returns a pauper having frittered his inheritance away. He returns in repentance expecting nothing more than to be his father's servant. The father has yearned for his son's return. He runs to greet him with loving open arms. A great celebration is prepared.

The reaction of the elder son brings us right back to the response of the Pharisees. Jesus reaches out to sinners and celebrates when they repent. Jesus warns his listeners, (and us) not to feel self righteous or act as though we are better than others. We must all rely on God's mercy and forgiveness.

 MEDITATIO:

- What aspects of these parables strike you most?
- Consider the attitude of the Pharisees compared to the shepherd, the woman and the father in these parables. What can we learn from this?
- Meditate on this verse:
  'This is a true saying, to be completely accepted and believed; Christ Jesus came into the world to save sinners.' 1 Timothy 1:15

 ORATIO:

Use the words of Psalm 51 as a personal prayer. Thank God for his great mercy.

Pray for the 'lost sheep' to return to Jesus. The Holy Spirit may bring someone specific to mind as you pray.

 CONTEMPLATIO:

Consider the role of the shepherd and the lengths that he will go to look after his sheep. Allow the love of our Great Shepherd to enfold you.

USE YOUR TALENTS WISELY

Luke 16:1-13

¹ Jesus said to his disciples, "There was once a rich man who had a servant who managed his property. The rich man was told that the manager was wasting his master's money, ² so he called him in and said, 'What is this I hear about you? Hand in a complete account of your handling of my property, because you cannot be my manager any longer.' ³ The servant said to himself, 'My master is going to dismiss me from my job. What shall I do? I am not strong enough to dig ditches, and I am ashamed to beg. ⁴ Now I know what I will do! Then when my job is gone, I shall have friends who will welcome me in their homes.'

⁵ "So he called in all the people who were in debt to his master. He asked the first one, 'How much do you owe my master?' ⁶ 'One hundred barrels of olive oil,' he answered. 'Here is your account,' the manager told him; 'sit down and write fifty.' ⁷ Then he asked another one, 'And you – how much do you owe?' 'A thousand sacks of wheat,' he answered. 'Here is your account,' the manager told him; 'write 800.'

⁸ "As a result the master of this dishonest manager praised him for doing such a shrewd thing; because the people of this world are much more shrewd in handling their affairs than the people who belong to the light."

⁹ And Jesus went on to say, "And so I tell you: make friends for yourselves with worldly wealth, so that when it gives out, you will be welcomed in the eternal home. ¹⁰ Whoever is faithful in small matters will be faithful in large ones; whoever is dishonest in small matters will be dishonest in large ones. ¹¹ If, then, you have not been faithful in handling worldly wealth, how can you be trusted with true wealth? ¹² And if you have not been faithful with what belongs to someone else, who will give you what belongs to you?

¹³ "No servant can be the slave of two masters; such a servant will hate one and love the other or will be loyal to one and despise the other. You cannot serve both God and money."

Other Readings: Amos 8:4-7; Psalm 113:1-2, 4-8; 1 Timothy 2:1-8

 LECTIO:

This can be a difficult parable to interpret. As with all parables it is important to focus on the main lessons rather than get sidetracked by taking the illustration too far. This passage can be understood on various levels but we will concentrate on two main points.

Jesus encourages us to be faithful stewards of the talents and resources he has entrusted to us especially our money. We should use these gifts wisely or shrewdly. However it would be wrong to conclude that Jesus approves of dishonest means to achieve this, as other passages of Scripture – including today's reading from Amos – make clear.

The other important point is to keep an eye on who exactly is your master, what or who drives you? Are God's principles guiding our daily lives or are they being shaped more by TV and the media? Are we truly serving God or really just ourselves? Jesus makes it clear we have to make a choice – no one can serve two masters.

 # MEDITATIO:

- Consider whether God is your only master or whether you are also trying to serve other masters too. Think about who, or what, influences what you do and think each day.
- Consider how faithful and wise you are being with the resources God has entrusted to you.
- Ask God to show you any ways you could bless others with your time and possessions.

 # ORATIO:

Use 1 Timothy 2:1-8 as a basis for your prayers today. We are instructed to pray for our leaders and people in authority. Ask God to guide them and help them to use their power wisely. We are also called to pray for freedom to practise our faith. Why not also take this opportunity to pray for those living in countries where it is hard and dangerous to live as a Christian?

 # CONTEMPLATIO:

Read Amos 8:4-7 and consider God's heart for the poor and those who are exploited by others. Are there any practical ways you can respond?

CARING FOR THE POOR

Luke 16:19-31

[19] "There was once a rich man who dressed in the most expensive clothes and lived in great luxury every day. [20] There was also a poor man named Lazarus, covered with sores, who used to be brought to the rich man's door, [21] hoping to eat the bits of food that fell from the rich man's table. Even the dogs would come and lick his sores.

[22] "The poor man died and was carried by the angels to sit beside Abraham at the feast in heaven. The rich man died and was buried, [23] and in Hades, where he was in great pain, he looked up and saw Abraham, far away, with Lazarus at his side. [24] So he called out, 'Father Abraham! Take pity on me, and send Lazarus to dip his finger in some water and cool my tongue, because I am in great pain in this fire!'

[25] "But Abraham said, 'Remember, my son, that in your lifetime you were given all the good things, while Lazarus got all the bad things. But now he is enjoying himself here, while you are in pain. [26] Besides all that, there is a deep pit lying between us, so that those who want to cross over from here to you cannot do so, nor can anyone cross over to us from where you are.' [27] The rich man said, 'Then I beg you, father Abraham, send Lazarus to my father's house, [28] where I have five brothers. Let him go and warn them so that they, at least, will not come to this place of pain.'

[29] "Abraham said, 'Your brothers have Moses and the prophets to warn them; your brothers should listen to what they say.' [30] The rich man answered, 'That is not enough, father Abraham! But if someone were to rise from death and go to them, then they would turn from their sins.' [31] But Abraham said, 'If they will not listen to Moses and the prophets, they will not be convinced even if someone were to rise from death.'"

Other Readings: Amos 6:1, 4-7; Psalm 146:6-10; 1 Timothy 6:11-16

 LECTIO:

Last week we considered what it means to be a good steward of all that God gives us. Luke alone gives us this parable which develops Jesus' teaching further.

Wealth appears to have made this rich man blind. He had seen Lazarus in a pitiful state outside his luxurious home. He even knew Lazarus' name (verse 24). But he did absolutely nothing to help him.

All Jews would know that Moses and the prophets taught that the rich had a social responsibility to care for the poor. In his selfishness this rich man disobeyed God's law. It is ironic that later, never having lifted a finger to help Lazarus, he asks Abraham to tell Lazarus to help him!

In Hades, family bonds draw out some compassion from the rich man. He thinks of his brothers and asks Abraham to send Lazarus with a warning. He doesn't want them to end up with the same punishment as him. Abraham responds that they have Moses and the prophets to warn them. This isn't good enough for the rich man. He believes something more dramatic is needed – only someone rising from the dead will convince his family. Abraham gives a very telling reply, 'they will not be convinced even if someone were to rise from death' (verse 31).

Not long after these words were spoken Jesus himself died and rose from the dead. Abraham's insight proved accurate both then and now. Even a great miracle will not convince those who ignore the warnings of the Bible. Sadly, many today still refuse to believe in God's Son Jesus and to serve him as their loving Master.

MEDITATIO:

- What is God revealing to you from this passage? Are you obeying God's teaching in this area of your life?
- Consider whether you are taking seriously the call to help others in need. This may mean more than just giving money; spending time with someone may be just as precious.
- Compare this reading with the words of the apostle Paul in 1 Timothy 6:17-19.

ORATIO:

How is God's concern for the poor and disadvantaged revealed in Psalm 146? Pray about your own response to this concern and pray for all those working to bring relief to those in need.

CONTEMPLATIO:

Spend some time considering the majesty of God described in 1 Timothy 6:15-16.

FAITH AND ACTIONS

Luke 17:5-10

⁵ The apostles said to the Lord, "Make our faith greater."

⁶ The Lord answered, "If you had faith as big as a mustard seed, you could say to this mulberry tree, 'Pull yourself up by the roots and plant yourself in the sea!' and it would obey you.

⁷ "Suppose one of you has a servant who is ploughing or looking after the sheep. When he comes in from the field, do you tell him to hurry and eat his meal? ⁸ Of course not! Instead, you say to him, 'Get my supper ready, then put on your apron and wait on me while I eat and drink; after that you may have your meal.' ⁹ The servant does not deserve thanks for obeying orders, does he? ¹⁰ It is the same with you; when you have done all you have been told to do, say, 'We are ordinary servants; we have only done our duty.' "

Other Readings: Habakkuk 1:2-3, 2:2-4; Psalm 95:1-2, 6-9; 2 Timothy 1:6-8, 13-14

 LECTIO:

Jesus packs a lot of teaching into these few short sentences. There are two themes: the first two verses concern faith and the later verses are about servanthood.

We begin with the disciples asking for faith. It is helpful to put their request in context. In the verses preceding today's Gospel reading the disciples have had a lesson about forgiveness and the consequence of causing someone else to lose faith. Forgiving someone three times was considered honourable according to Jewish tradition at the time. But Jesus calls his disciples to forgive as often as is needed. The disciples realise that following Jesus will demand far more than they are able to give so they ask for more faith.

Jesus replies that what is important is to have a genuine faith in God. It doesn't matter how small this may be; whenever genuine faith is present remarkable things can and do happen.

Jesus then talks about the idea of servanthood. The heart of his teaching is that God deserves our service simply because of who he is. God owes us nothing. We owe him everything. The worldly attitude is to expect a reward for what you do. It's a great temptation to expect God to bless us in some way when we serve him. Jesus makes it clear this attitude is wrong. Taking pleasure in serving him out of gratitude and love is all the reward we need.

To be servants of God means above all to be people of faith. Right attitudes in serving God keep us humble and help guard us against pride.

 # MEDITATIO:

- Which of these verses speak most clearly to you at this point in your life?
- Do you see yourself as God's servant? Think about the reasons why you serve God. Are you satisfied with serving him out of love and gratitude, or do you look for praise from others?
- Spend a little time with your eyes fixed on the Lord. Let him soften your heart and draw you close to him so that your faith, service and gratitude may grow.

 # ORATIO:

Prayerfully consider your response to God from this reading and your meditation.

In today's reading from Paul's letter to Timothy, the apostle encourages the young evangelist to keep alive the gift God gave him. This can speak to us too. Ask the Holy Spirit to nurture these precious gifts of power, love and self control, enabling you to live out your life in humble service to God. The Holy Spirit will also help you endure when times are hard.

 # CONTEMPLATIO:

Consider this verse from the apostle Paul's letter to the Romans:

> 'So then, my brothers and sisters, because of God's great mercy to us I appeal to you: offer yourselves as a living sacrifice to God, dedicated to his service and pleasing to him. This is the true worship that you should offer.' Romans 12:1

ALWAYS BE THANKFUL

Luke 17:11-19

¹¹ As Jesus made his way to Jerusalem, he went along the border between Samaria and Galilee. ¹² He was going into a village when he was met by ten men suffering from a dreaded skin disease. They stood at a distance ¹³ and shouted, "Jesus! Master! Take pity on us!"

¹⁴ Jesus saw them and said to them, "Go and let the priests examine you."

On the way they were made clean. ¹⁵ When one of them saw that he was healed, he came back, praising God in a loud voice. ¹⁶ He threw himself to the ground at Jesus' feet and thanked him. The man was a Samaritan. ¹⁷ Jesus said, "There were ten men who were healed; where are the other nine? ¹⁸ Why is this foreigner the only one who came back to give thanks to God?" ¹⁹ And Jesus said to him, "Get up and go; your faith has made you well."

Other Readings: 2 Kings 5:14-17; Psalm 98:1-4; 2 Timothy 2:8-13

 LECTIO:

In today's Gospel reading Jesus gives us an important lesson in being thankful for God's blessings.

Jesus is on his way to Jerusalem to face his crucifixion and resurrection. Standing at a distance on the outskirts of a village ten men with a dreaded skin disease cry out to him, 'Jesus! Master! Take pity on us!' (verse 13).

The plight of people suffering from leprosy and other skin diseases in Jesus' day was very harsh indeed. They were forced to leave their family and friends and live in exile away from the rest of the community. They had to fend for themselves alongside others in the same condition.

They were cut off from the religious life of the community and considered 'spiritually unclean'. Some even believed that their disease was a punishment from God. Their situation was miserable, their prospects were bleak and there was little hope. The only way back to a normal life was if the skin disease cleared up and the priests certified it.

No wonder these men cried to Jesus for help. Jesus simply tells them to let the priests examine them. They all obey Jesus' instructions and on the way to the priests the miracle takes place. All ten are healed.

As soon as one of the group discovers he has been healed he rushes back to thank Jesus and give praise to God. Did he talk to the other nine before returning? We are not told. But we are told that this man was a Samaritan.

The other nine were presumably all Jewish. Jesus was a Jewish teacher. The Jews looked down on the Samaritans and regarded them as religious heretics. The very person they would have least expected to show his gratitude is in fact the only one who gives thanks to God.

Jesus' final words to the Samaritan are significant. The word translated 'Get up' has several meanings; early Christians would have understood a reference to resurrection or new life. Ten lepers were healed but only the Samaritan is told his faith has made him well. Perhaps Jesus is referring to spiritual as well as physical healing.

 MEDITATIO:

- How does this passage speak to you?
- Why do you think the nine that were also healed didn't return to thank Jesus? Have you ever received an answer to prayer but forgot to thank God before doing anything else?
- How can we avoid taking God's blessings for granted? Is there a danger that we can sometimes feel we 'deserve' God's blessing because of something we have done?

 ORATIO:

Think about all the ways God has been good to you. Write them down and read your list through each day this week. Respond to God with thanks and praise. The Holy Spirit may well remind you of more things as the week progresses. Ask God to help you to always be grateful for all he has done in your life.

Choose a Psalm each day this week to help you express your praise to God.

 CONTEMPLATIO:

Consider these verses from Philippians 4:4, 6-7:

'May you always be joyful in your union with the Lord. I say it again: rejoice! Don't worry about anything, but in all your prayers ask God for what you need, always asking him with a thankful heart. And God's peace, which is far beyond human understanding, will keep your hearts and minds safe in union with Christ Jesus.'

DON'T GIVE UP

Luke 18:1-8

[1] Then Jesus told his disciples a parable to teach them that they should always pray and never become discouraged. [2] "In a certain town there was a judge who neither feared God nor respected people. [3] And there was a widow in that same town who kept coming to him and pleading for her rights, saying, 'Help me against my opponent!' [4] For a long time the judge refused to act, but at last he said to himself, 'Even though I don't fear God or respect people, [5] yet because of all the trouble this widow is giving me, I will see to it that she gets her rights. If I don't, she will keep on coming and finally wear me out!' "

[6] And the Lord continued, "Listen to what that corrupt judge said. [7] Now, will God not judge in favour of his own people who cry to him day and night for help? Will he be slow to help them? [8] I tell you, he will judge in their favour and do it quickly. But will the Son of Man find faith on earth when he comes?"

Other Readings: Exodus 17:8-13; Psalm 121; 2 Timothy 3:14 – 4:2

 LECTIO:

Jesus is a master at making complex ideas clear. Here he uses a simple story to explain the importance of perseverance, which he links to prayer.

The widow who appeals to the judge is seeking justice. She simply wants him to uphold her rights so her opponent complies with the law. But for some reason the judge keeps refusing to hear her case.

Eventually the judge gives in, not because it is the right thing to do, but because he realises this woman just won't give up. He can't face the thought of her coming to him time after time so he concedes and judges in her favour.

Jesus then contrasts the behaviour of the corrupt judge with God. The differences are so great it is like comparing black and white. Jesus assures us that God will judge in favour of his people and he will do it swiftly. Why? Because God is good and just. So we needn't fear asking for God's help because he will surely answer (first half of verse 8).

In the second half of verse 8 Jesus asks another question: 'But will the Son of Man find faith on earth when he comes?' What does this have to do with persistence in prayer?

Perhaps Jesus is saying that persevering prayer is sustained by faith. If you believe God loves you then you don't stop praying, even if God does not answer immediately.

More importantly, Jesus implies that his return may be longer than some expect. So there is a link with persistence and endurance especially for the faithful who pray.

Persistent prayer encourages a faithful hope and that is where Jesus started his parable. It links to the verses in Luke 21:34-36 about remaining watchful in prayer because no one knows the time when Jesus will return. And this was just as true for the disciples as it is for us today.

MEDITATIO:

- Think of times when you have had to wait a long time for God's answer to your prayers. What encouraged you to keep persevering and not give up?
- Why do you think God doesn't always answer our prayers immediately or sometimes says 'no'?
- Consider the parallel between this passage and Matt 7:7-11 which also teaches about persistence in prayer: 'Bad as you are, you know how to give good things to your children. How much more will your Father in heaven give good things to those who ask him!'

ORATIO:

Psalm 121:2 reminds us that, 'My help will come from the Lord who made heaven and earth.'

Why not bring the things that concern you to God again in prayer today? Ask for his help not to give up as you wait to see his response. Give thanks that the all powerful creator of the universe will not fail us.

CONTEMPLATIO:

Consider Paul's words in 2 Timothy 3:14 – 4.2, particularly verses 16-17 below. What do they mean to you?

'All Scripture is inspired by God and is useful for teaching the truth, rebuking error, correcting faults, and giving instruction for right living, so that the person who serves God may be fully qualified and equipped to do every kind of good deed.'

STAYING RIGHT WITH GOD

Luke 18:9-14

⁹ Jesus also told this parable to people who were sure of their own goodness and despised everybody else. ¹⁰ "Once there were two men who went up to the Temple to pray: one was a Pharisee, the other a tax collector.

¹¹ "The Pharisee stood apart by himself and prayed, 'I thank you, God, that I am not greedy, dishonest, or an adulterer, like everybody else. I thank you that I am not like that tax collector over there. ¹² I fast two days a week, and I give you a tenth of all my income.'

¹³ "But the tax collector stood at a distance and would not even raise his face to heaven, but beat on his breast and said, 'God, have pity on me, a sinner!' ¹⁴ I tell you," said Jesus, "the tax collector, and not the Pharisee, was in the right with God when he went home. For all who make themselves great will be humbled, and all who humble themselves will be made great."

Other Readings: Ecclesiasticus 35:12-14, 16-19; Psalm 34:1-2, 16-18, 22; 2 Timothy 4:6-8, 16-18

 LECTIO:

Jesus told this parable originally 'to people who were sure of their own goodness and despised everybody else' (verse 9). That is the key to understanding this passage.

Much of Jesus' teaching in Luke's Gospel opens the doors of the Kingdom of God to let in sinners who are willing to repent. By contrast the Pharisees seem set on keeping sinners out.

Jesus uses the behaviour of the Pharisee and the tax collector to make his point clear. For the people gathered around Jesus the characteristics of the two personalities he is using are well known.

The Pharisees are considered the 'professionals' when it comes to prayer. What they didn't know about religious law and how to observe it wasn't really worth knowing. They are officially 'good'.

But the tax collector is assumed to be corrupt – what else could he be since he was colluding with the pagan Romans occupying their country? Tax collectors were the puppets of the Roman authorities; they collected taxes from their own people and made themselves rich in the process by taking far more tax than they should.

As the parable unfolds Jesus' purpose in using these two characters becomes clearer. The Pharisee prays in a proud boastful way, only seeing what he does right and others do wrong. He forgets to confess his sins. The tax collector does the opposite. He knows he needs God's forgiveness, and in acknowledging his sinfulness before God he is ready and able to receive God's forgiveness and grace. The Pharisee is not and so does not receive God's grace.

We are challenged in the same way. Every single person has sinned and each one needs God's forgiveness.

The Pharisees actually sought to bring a religious renewal among the Jews of Jesus's own time. Sadly they failed to accept Jesus' message. They did not see him as the one sent by God to save humanity. They opposed Jesus, seeing him as an impostor, and refused to believe in him.

 MEDITATIO:

- Consider the reasons why God hates sin.
- What is your attitude to sin in your own life? Do you take it seriously and seek forgiveness? Or do you excuse it, or compare yourself with others and think you are better than them?
- Consider 1 John 1:8-9:
  'If we say we have no sin, we deceive ourselves, and there is no truth in us. But if we confess our sins to God, he will keep his promise and do what is right: he will forgive us our sins and purify us from all our wrongdoing.'
  Do you ask for pardon for your sins? Catholics know that they can confess their sins to their priest and receive forgiveness from God.
- We can easily fall into the trap of judging others who fall short of our own standards. Why is this dangerous? How can we avoid it? What attitude should we have?

 ORATIO:

Reflect on today's Gospel reading. Let God reveal any areas of sin that you need to put right. Consider whether you have taken God's forgiveness for granted. Give thanks for God's mercy and acknowledge your dependence on him.

 CONTEMPLATIO:

Use Psalms 34 and 51 to enrich your time with God today. Consider his great faithfulness and mercy.

TRUE HAPPINESS

Matthew 5:1-12

¹Jesus saw the crowds and went up a hill, where he sat down. His disciples gathered round him, ²and he began to teach them:

³"Happy are those who know they are spiritually poor;
   the Kingdom of heaven belongs to them!
⁴Happy are those who mourn;
   God will comfort them!
⁵Happy are those who are humble;
   they will receive what God has promised!
⁶Happy are those whose greatest desire is to do what God requires;
   God will satisfy them fully!
⁷Happy are those who are merciful to others;
   God will be merciful to them!
⁸Happy are the pure in heart;
   they will see God!
⁹Happy are those who work for peace;
   God will call them his children!
¹⁰Happy are those who are persecuted because they do what God requires;
   the Kingdom of heaven belongs to them!

¹¹"Happy are you when people insult you and persecute you and tell all kinds of evil lies against you because you are my followers. ¹²Be happy and glad, for a great reward is kept for you in heaven. This is how the prophets who lived before you were persecuted.

Other Readings: Revelation 7:2-4, 9-14; Psalm 24:1-6; 1 John 3:1-3

 LECTIO:

Matthew's Gospel is structured around five major teachings of Jesus, mainly to his disciples. The first of these is centred on what is often called the Sermon on the Mount or the Beatitudes.

The radical differences between the 'kingdom of heaven' – Jesus' rule as Lord and King being established on earth - and the earthly kingdom lie at the heart of this sermon.

Jesus sums up the lifestyle and attitudes that bring true happiness, or blessing, in nine statements. These are very different from what the world would say brings happiness. In fact you could almost say the happiness described above is the direct opposite of what people in the world think makes them happy.

In some translations the word 'blessed' is used instead of happiness. Another translation could be 'contented'. There is a contentment or fulfilment that comes from following and serving God rather than just pleasing ourselves.

This short list of nine beatitudes sums up the core values of gospel living. Some are also listed in the Old Testament but Jesus draws all the threads together to provide us with an excellent reference point to guide our lives. The focus is always on our relationship with God and with others. The saints known and unknown learned this, so can we. True happiness will only be found living out these Beatitudes.

 # MEDITATIO:

- Which of the Beatitudes stands out for you the most?
- Which do you find most challenging? Consider how you might put more of Jesus' teaching into practice in the coming weeks.
- Look back to the Sixth Sunday in Ordinary Time (14th February) when we considered Luke's account of this teaching. What strikes you when you compare these two accounts?

 # ORATIO:

Read these Beatitudes through slowly several times. Ask the Holy Spirit to speak to you. Make a note of what you feel God is saying to you through this teaching. Ask God to help you in the areas where you feel particularly weak.

Read Psalm 24:1-6. Use these verses during your time of prayer today.

 # CONTEMPLATIO:

'Think of the love that the Father has lavished on us, by letting us be called God's children;' 1 John 3:1 *Jerusalem Bible*

Reflect on the depth of God's love for you that this verse reveals. Make your own response to God.

RESURRECTION HOPE

Luke 20:27-38

²⁷ Then some Sadducees, who say that people will not rise from death, came to Jesus and said, ²⁸ "Teacher, Moses wrote this law for us: 'If a man dies and leaves a wife but no children, that man's brother must marry the widow so that they can have children who will be considered the dead man's children.' ²⁹ Once there were seven brothers; the eldest got married and died without having children. ³⁰ Then the second one married the woman, ³¹ and then the third. The same thing happened to all seven – they died without having children. ³² Last of all, the woman died. ³³ Now, on the day when the dead rise to life, whose wife will she be? All seven of them had married her."

³⁴ Jesus answered them, "The men and women of this age marry, ³⁵ but the men and women who are worthy to rise from death and live in the age to come will not then marry. ³⁶ They will be like angels and cannot die. They are the children of God, because they have risen from death. ³⁷ And Moses clearly proves that the dead are raised to life. In the passage about the burning bush he speaks of the Lord as 'the God of Abraham, the God of Isaac, and the God of Jacob.' ³⁸ He is the God of the living, not of the dead, for to him all are alive."

Other Readings: 2 Maccabees 7:1-2, 9-14; Psalm 17:1, 5-6, 8, 15; 2 Thessalonians 2:16-3:5

 LECTIO:

We begin with the Sadducees. They were an influential religious group when Jesus was on earth. Their power stemmed from being in charge of the Temple in Jerusalem. They based their religious life and faith on just the first five books of the Bible, the Pentateuch, which sets out the Law.

They didn't believe in bodily resurrection, which Jesus and the Pharisees upheld (Acts 23:6-9). So to try and prove their point they put this absurd question to Jesus. It is based on the 'Levirate Law' (Deuteronomy 25:5-10). If a husband died without an heir his brother was required to marry the widow to protect family property.

Jesus replies that resurrection life will not be the same as the life we live today. Those 'who are worthy to rise from death' will be like angels and will live forever (verses 34-36). So there will be no need for marriage or for children to continue the family line.

We are not given many details about our resurrection body. We do know that the disciples recognised Jesus after his resurrection, even if others like the two disciples on the road to Emmaus didn't recognise him immediately (Luke 24:13-35).

Jesus concludes his argument by quoting from a book that the Sadducees accepted as authoritative, Exodus. He cites Moses as proof that the dead are raised to life. When God speaks to Moses from the burning bush he reveals himself as the God of Abraham, Isaac and Jacob (Exodus 3:6).

The patriarchs are presented as alive. First century Jews would have understood that the patriarchs hadn't yet literally risen from the dead but 'lived' with God awaiting their final resurrection. God is the God of the living not of the dead.

 MEDITATIO:

- Resurrection is a cornerstone of Christian faith. If Jesus wasn't raised from the dead then we would have no foundation to hope that there is life after death. Are you confident in this hope? Read the apostle Paul's argument for the resurrection in 1 Corinthians 15.

 ORATIO:

Pray these verses from 2 Thessalonians and bring any fears to God:

'May our Lord Jesus Christ himself and God our Father, who loved us and in his grace gave us unfailing courage and a firm hope, encourage you and strengthen you always to do good and say what is good.
May the Lord lead you into a greater understanding of God's love and the endurance that is given by Christ.' 2 Thessalonians 2:16-17, 3:5

 CONTEMPLATIO:

Consider this encouragement from Philippians 3:20-21:

'We, however, are citizens of heaven, we eagerly wait for the coming of our Saviour, the Lord Jesus Christ, to come from heaven. He will change our weak mortal bodies and make them like his own glorious body, using that power by which he is able to bring all things under his rule.'

STAND FIRM

Luke 21:5-19

⁵ Some of the disciples were talking about the Temple, how beautiful it looked with its fine stones and the gifts offered to God. Jesus said, ⁶ "All this you see – the time will come when not a single stone here will be left in its place; every one will be thrown down."

⁷ "Teacher," they asked, "when will this be? And what will happen in order to show that the time has come for it to take place?"

⁸ Jesus said, "Be on guard; don't be deceived. Many men, claiming to speak for me, will come and say, 'I am he!' and, 'The time has come!' But don't follow them. ⁹ Don't be afraid when you hear of wars and revolutions; such things must happen first, but they do not mean that the end is near."

¹⁰ He went on to say, "Countries will fight each other; kingdoms will attack one another. ¹¹ There will be terrible earthquakes, famines, and plagues everywhere; there will be strange and terrifying things coming from the sky. ¹² Before all these things take place, however, you will be arrested and persecuted; you will be handed over to be tried in synagogues and be put in prison; you will be brought before kings and rulers for my sake. ¹³ This will be your chance to tell the Good News. ¹⁴ Make up your minds beforehand not to worry about how you will defend yourselves, ¹⁵ because I will give you such words and wisdom that none of your enemies will be able to refute or contradict what you say. ¹⁶ You will be handed over by your parents, your brothers, your relatives, and your friends; and some of you will be put to death. ¹⁷ Everyone will hate you because of me. ¹⁸ But not a single hair from your heads will be lost. ¹⁹ Stand firm, and you will save yourselves.

Other Readings: Malachi 3:19-20; Psalm 98:5-9; 2 Thessalonians 3:7-12

 LECTIO:

This is Luke's version of Jesus' end of the world, or apocalyptic, teaching. We find similar passages in Matthew and Mark. But each writer emphasises different aspects of Jesus' teaching according to the needs of their particular community.

Luke writes to those living away from Palestine. It was a time of war with Rome. Luke probably wrote his Gospel after Jerusalem and the temple were destroyed by the Romans in AD 70. This part of Jesus' prophetic words would therefore already have been fulfilled when the early Christians read Luke's account.

In addition to prophesying the destruction of Jerusalem and the persecution of the early Christian church, Jesus also makes a link to the end of the world (verses 10-11, 25-36). So his warnings remain equally important for us today – when persecution comes because of our faith, don't be surprised. Jesus has warned us in advance, persecution is to be expected.

And if persecution comes knocking at our door we need to stand firm. We must endure, remain patient and stand firm. God is still with us even if family or friends reject or betray us.

Luke knew about the reality of persecution. By the time he wrote his Gospel Peter and Paul had been killed as had many other Christians.

Jesus' words are a reminder that persecution happens and takes many forms. It is a practical fact in many parts of the world today. Some Christians are driven from their homes, their jobs and some lose their lives. The message is still the same: stand firm. God loves you and will not abandon you.

MEDITATIO:

- What types of persecution have you experienced because of your faith?
- Perhaps you have been insulted, embarrassed or ridiculed. How do you react in these situations? What did you say or do? How did you bear witness to Jesus?

ORATIO:

Pray that God will give you the courage and strength to stand firm in the face of any persecution that might come your way so that you bear a good witness to God.

Pray for Christians living in countries where persecution is severe. Pray for those who are in prison because of their faith or who have been rejected by their families.

CONTEMPLATIO:

'... sing together with joy before the Lord, because he comes to rule the earth. He will rule the peoples of the world with justice and fairness.'
Psalm 98:8b-9

Read the rest of Psalm 98 and spend some time reflecting on God's mighty power and justice.

THE HEAVENLY KING

Luke 23:35-43

³⁵ The people stood there watching while the Jewish leaders jeered at him: "He saved others; let him save himself if he is the Messiah whom God has chosen!"

³⁶ The soldiers also mocked him: they came up to him and offered him cheap wine, ³⁷ and said, "Save yourself if you are the king of the Jews!"

³⁸ Above him were written these words: "This is the King of the Jews."

³⁹ One of the criminals hanging there hurled insults at him: "Aren't you the Messiah? Save yourself and us!"

⁴⁰ The other one, however, rebuked him, saying, "Don't you fear God? You received the same sentence he did. ⁴¹ Ours, however, is only right, because we are getting what we deserve for what we did; but he has done no wrong." ⁴² And he said to Jesus, "Remember me, Jesus, when you come as King!"

⁴³ Jesus said to him, "I promise you that today you will be in Paradise with me."

Other Readings: 2 Samuel 5:1-3; Psalm 122:1-5; Colossians 1:12-20

 LECTIO:

We stand before the cross today. Jesus is dying in agony alongside two criminals. The leaders are jeering and mocking him for claiming to be the Messiah but not being able to even save himself! The Roman soldiers are also pouring scorn on this so-called 'King of the Jews'.

In marked contrast Luke provides us with a fascinating conversation between Jesus and one of the criminals. He is the only Gospel writer to record this life changing exchange.

One of the criminals joins the taunts ridiculing Jesus' Messianic claim. The other criminal rebukes him. He recognises two vital things. Firstly, something the Jewish leaders failed to see, that Jesus 'has done no wrong' (verse 41), he is innocent and doesn't deserve this punishment. Secondly, something the disciples were desperately hoping was true, that this wasn't the end, Jesus would be returning and when he did it would be as King (verse 42).

The God-fearing criminal accepted he deserved to be punished for his actions, expressed faith in Jesus and threw himself on God's mercy, knowing this was his only hope. Jesus responds as he always does to genuine faith and cries for mercy, with the gift of salvation.

MEDITATIO:

- Pause at the foot of the cross. Acknowledge your sinfulness. Rejoice that the grace of God is available to redeem sinners like us.
- How did you recognise Jesus as your Saviour? Were you given a blinding moment of grace when you knew the truth like the criminal? Or has your understanding been a gradual process bringing you to faith over months or years?
- Think ahead to when Jesus will return in power and glory as King of Kings and Lord of Lords. Meditate on this glorious hope.

 ORATIO:

Spend some time giving thanks because Jesus took the punishment for our sins on the cross. We too can receive forgiveness and inherit eternal life, and all by God's gracious gift; we can do nothing to deserve or earn it.

 CONTEMPLATIO:

Consider your wonderful Saviour as revealed in Colossians 1:15-20. Read these verses several times and let them minister to your soul.

> [15]'Christ is the visible likeness of the invisible God. He is the firstborn Son, superior to all created things. [16]For through him God created everything in heaven and on earth, the seen and the unseen things, including spiritual powers, lords, rulers, and authorities. God created the whole universe through him and for him. [17]Christ existed before all things, and in union with him all things have their proper place. [18]He is the head of his body, the church; he is the source of the body's life. He is the firstborn Son, who was raised from death, in order that he alone might have the first place in all things. [19]For it was by God's own decision that the Son has in himself the full nature of God. [20]Through the Son, then, God decided to bring the whole universe back to himself. God made peace through his Son's blood on the cross and so brought back to himself all things, both on earth and in heaven.'

UNITED
BIBLE
SOCIETIES

The United Bible Societies (UBS) is a global fellowship of 145 national Bible Societies operating in over 200 countries and territories. Collectively, the Fellowship is the biggest translator, publisher and distributor of the Bible in the world. Bible Societies are not affiliated to any one Christian Church. They work in partnership with all Christian Churches and many international organisations.

Translating the Bible is at the heart of Bible Society work and our translation policy ensures that we have translation guidelines that are acceptable to the Catholic, Protestant and Orthodox Churches. Bible Societies are also committed to finding new and imaginative ways to draw people into the Bible so that it is central in the material, cultural and spiritual lives of people everywhere. For more details visit: **www.biblesociety.org**

These *lectio divina* outlines are also available in Albanian, Dutch, French, Greek, Maltese, Portuguese, Slovak, Slovenian, Spanish and other languages. For full details visit: **www.wordforliving.org**

The Scottish Bible Society seeks, under God, to put the Scriptures into people's hands and hearts. We work so that people can have the Bible in a language they understand, a form they can access and at an affordable price, to aid genuine encounters with God.
The Scottish Bible Society, 7 Hampton Terrace,
Edinburgh EH12 5XU. Tel 0131 347 9809
www.scottishbiblesociety.org

"Your word is a lamp to guide me
and a light for my path."

Psalm 119:105
Good News Bible